DATE DUE

OPPORTUNITIES IN

TRAVEL
CAREERS

By Robert Scott Milne

VOCATIONAL GUIDANCE MANUALS, INC.

Louisville, Kentucky

Copyright © 1976
Vocational Guidance Manuals, Inc.
A subsidiary of the Courier-Journal
and Louisville Times Company.
620 South Fifth Street
Louisville, Kentucky 40202

Manufactured in the
United States of America

Library of Congress Catalog Card Number 75–32612

ISBN Number   0–89022–209–6 Hardcover
                    0–89022–027–1 Paper

ABOUT THE AUTHOR

Robert Scott Milne has been a full-time free-lance travel writer since 1972. Before that he was an encyclopedia editor for 16 years, first on *Collier's Encyclopedia* and then on *Encyclopedia Americana.* During most of his encyclopedia period, however, he was a moonlight travel writer for newspapers and magazines. He has been an active member of the Society of American Travel Writers since 1966, works on the Society's Publications Committee, and is an officer of its Freelancers Council.

Among the publications that have published his travel articles are: New York *Times, Post, News,* and *Herald Tribune;* Chicago *Tribune, Youth Beat,* and numerous other newspapers; *Seventeen, Atlantic Monthly, Argosy, Vista USA, Chevron USA, Relax, Modern Bride, Off Duty, Applause, Rx Sports and Travel,* and many other magazines. In addition to thousands of articles he has written for the two encyclopedias mentioned above, Mr. Milne has contributed to *The New Book of Knowledge* and its *Annual, Lands and Peoples, The Wonderland of Knowledge, United Educators Encyclopedia,* the multilingual Swiss-published encyclopedia, *Discovery 2000, Americana Annual,* and *World Topics Yearbook.* Among the books to which he has contributed are: *Around the World With the Experts, The Great Escape,* and *Mrs. Siu's Chinese Cookbook.*

Since 1972 he has maintained his own office—the envy of the travel-writing fraternity—in The Plaza Hotel in New York City. With his Vienna-born wife, Gaby, who is a musician, he lives in Elmsford, New York. They share the house with three dogs and a parrot, Canaima, purchased from Indians in a Venezuela jungle camp. The Milnes travel extensively, by every means available, including their camper.

TABLE OF CONTENTS

Historical background. How big is the travel industry?
Personal travel. Opportunities for women. The broad
variety of travel jobs.

Flight attendants. Airline pilots and copilots. Flight
engineers. Aircraft mechanics. Flight dispatchers.
Ticket agents, reservation agents, and clerks. Air
traffic controllers.

Passenger service representatives. Reservation and
information clerks. Conductors. Engineers and firemen. Station agents. Clerks. Salaries and employment
benefits.

DEDICATION

And now I see with eye serene,
The very pulse of the machine;
A being breathing thoughtful breath,
A traveler betwixt life and death;
The reason firm, the temperate will,
Endurance, foresight, strength, and skill;
A perfect woman, nobly planned,
To warn, to comfort, and command;
And yet a spirit still, and bright
With something of angelic light.

—William Wordsworth

For Gaby, the pulse of my machine.

PREFACE–THOUGHTS ON TOURISM

President Gerald R. Ford:

"Never before has tourism had such an impact on so many of our national interests. It is a vital aspect of our nation's economy and, more than ever, an important factor in our relations with other countries. Tourism has growing value as a source of foreign currency. It can appreciably strengthen the vitality of our economy at a time when this is our primary national task."

William D. Toohey, president, Discover America Travel Organizations:

"Over the next decade, opportunities for employment within the tourism industry are expected to increase significantly, offering an unlimited future for a variety of Americans with varied and widely divergent job skills.

"It is difficult to predict precisely what travel career opportunities will exist, when considering that between 1970 and 1980, tourism employment is expected to enjoy a growth rate twice as great as that projected for total nonagricultural employment in the United States.

"We can expect that as Americans gain additional leisure time in the years ahead and learn to allocate this time, even more employment opportunities will develop in the diverse mix of activities we call the tourism industry. These include the airlines, automobile manufacturers, bus operators, rail lines, accommodations, state and city tourism offices, attractions, outdoor recreational companies, ski area operators, car rental firms, retail travel agents, tour wholesalers, and tour brokers, to name but a few.

"In addition, employment opportunities will also be created in those industries which support travel and tourism, including the luggage industry, camera and film companies, and clothing manufacturers.

"In short, the future of tourism employment is virtually unlimited in the context of a new leisure ethic in the United States which, I believe, will continue to develop as we move to and through the 1980s."

Dr. Samuel I. Porrath, founder and chairman, The Institute of Transportation, Travel, and Tourism, Niagara University, New York:

"TTT (travel, transportation, and tourism) is an interfusion of industries that creates one of the world's most fascinating businesses. TTT is an amalgam of intercontinental enterprises, all of them growing rapidly and expanding daily, thus promising a strong, energetic future to those embracing it. TTT industries look for dedicated, management-level, university trained, academically prepared professionals equipped with the proper backgrounds for their multifaceted universal interests."

Dr. Douglas C. Frechtling, director, United States Travel Data Center:

"Six million Americans travel each day. These travelers need to be fed, housed, entertained, and transported. The travel industry rose to meet those needs of the public.

"Tourism is essential as a source of jobs and governmental revenue, and in this way it benefits people. Four million jobs are produced by tourism and $61 billion is spent annually on travel in the United States."

ACKNOWLEDGMENTS

This book would not have been possible without the whole-hearted cooperation of many people in all facets of the travel industry. For information, pictures, statements about the future of the industry, and many other kinds of assistance, the author sincerely thanks the following persons: Eunice Juckett, travel writer; Christine Maddox, senior editor at Vocational Guidance Manuals; Janet Luoma of The Plaza in New York; Harry Mullikin, president of Western International Hotels; Marguerite Allen, senior vice president, Robert F. Warner (Distinguished Hotels of the World); William D. Toohey, president of Discover America Travel Organizations (DATO); Jason King, operator of Yours in Travel Personnel Agency in New York; Dr. Samuel I. Porrath, founder and chairman of the Transportation, Travel and Tourism Institute (TTT) at Niagara University; Albert E. Kudrle of the American Hotel & Motel Association; Kathy M. Burns of Monterey Peninsula College; Richard J. Sullivan, registrar at Notre Dame; Irving W. Morrill, coordinator of the TTT Program at Adelphi University; David H. Lobb of American Airlines; Alan B. Wayne of United Airlines; Harriette S. Parker of Delta Airlines; Jeff Kreindler of Pan American World Airways; Robert Randell of Trans World Airlines; the late Eugene Du Bois of Eastern Airlines; John F. McLeod of Amtrak; Patrick R. Sheridan, president of Gray Line Sight-Seeing Companies; Gene Teeling of Greyhound Lines; Kim M. Arnone of Continental Trailways; Daniel Z. Henkin, vice president of the Air Transport Association; Patricia Rose and Sheridan H. Garth of Thomas Cook & Son; Monica Burke of Inter-Continental Hotels; public relations specialist Linda Kundell; Edwina Arnold of Club Méditerranée; Hella M. Rothwell of Island Holidays Resorts in Hawaii; Philip D. Shea and Al Banks of The Sheraton Corporation; James L. Shanahan of Americana Hotels; Jacques C. Cossé of Hilton Hotels Corporation; Philip Miles of Loews Hotels; Lis K. Brewer and Karen Weiner of Hilton International; John W. Hill, board chairman of Hill & Knowlton; Jafar Jafari, editor of *Annals of Tourism Research* at the University of Wisconsin–Stout, in Menomonie, Wisconsin; Debbie Swanson of the American Society of Travel Agents (ASTA); Robert Jackson of the United States Travel Service in the Department of Commerce; and for much forbearance and patience while I wrote this book, my wife Gaby.

A WORD ABOUT SEX

The masculine pronouns are being used in this book for succinctness and are intended to refer to both females and males.

CHAPTER 1

TRANSPORTATION, TRAVEL, AND TOURISM

Confusion is rampant as to the exact meanings of the words *transportation, travel,* and *tourism.* This confusion has been aggravated by the fact that in the period of America's early affluence, some of those who acquired riches before they acquired culture made themselves ridiculous by their uncouth manners, loud voices, and conspicuous consumption, particularly when they were traveling in Europe. As a result, many tourists preferred to be called *travelers,* and tourist agencies became *travel agencies;* tourist bureaus became *visitors bureaus,* and so forth.

Today, this artificial distinction has largely eroded away, and these words can now be used with their real meanings. A tourist no longer feels insulted if he is called a tourist, and numerous governmental offices call themselves tourist promotion bureaus.

Arbitrary but interesting definitions of these words are used at Niagara University (New York) in the Institute of Transportation, Travel and Tourism (TTT). At TTT, *transportation* is defined as the movement of goods; *travel* is defined as the movement of people; and *tourism* concerns the entire business of leisure travel and related supporting activities.

This manual concentrates on careers in all three of these broad fields, but selects those in which the work requires travel, direct service to travelers or vacationers, or promotion of travel and destinations. Thus, we shall discuss careers in the merchant marine because they entail travel, even though 97 percent of the workers on U.S. oceangoing ships are on tankers and freighters, and only three percent are on passenger ships. We shall omit consideration of jobs in such fields as aircraft and automobile manufacture and auto repair. They serve the traveling public, but not directly, and little or no travel is required for their work.

HISTORICAL BACKGROUND

Travel has always been an important feature of people's lives. Historically, this has been what we would classify today as business travel, concerned, in the most primitive sense, with staying alive—travel to obtain food. Then, working up the scale of civilization, travel became a means to promote trade, consolidate governments, and provide communication.

Great migrations of peoples took place after such disasters as lava flows or floods had devastated their lands. This was business travel of the purest sort—they had to find new lands that would support them. Nomads in semiarid lands seldom stayed long in one place because their grazing animals would soon consume all the vegetation, requiring them to move on. Many groups of people who herded animals, such as the Laplanders with their reindeer, moved twice every year between summer pastures and winter havens.

As people began to specialize in what they could grow or make or mine from the earth, trade developed. The first traveling salesmen were emissaries sent to find markets for goods and to arrange for caravans or ships to deliver these goods.

Military travel also developed early, as warlike tribes conquered peaceful ones and moved into their territories. As empires grew, men traveled ceaselessly between the capital and the farthest borders to supervise and carry orders and to impose the ruler's will. Regular messenger systems became fast and reliable as early as ancient times in Egypt, developing over the millennia into stagecoach and packetboat networks, the Pony Express, and modern diplomatic courier and postal systems.

The lure of adventure and travel has always been a dominating element in human recreation. Today, the travel industry employs a significant percentage of the U.S. work force in jobs as varied as they are numerous.

Thus, the stream of travelers has grown constantly—seamen, oxcart drivers, herdsmen, messengers, salesmen, armies, covered-wagon trains, all intent on carrying on their own work or someone else's.

Another kind of travel developed in medieval times—educational travel. A young man learning a craft was apprenticed to a master craftsman near home for a period of years to learn the basics, then he spent a year traveling to the workshops of masters of the craft in other countries, where he worked for a time to gain more skill and knowledge. Upon his return from his travels he was no longer an apprentice, but a journeyman—one who had traveled and learned. Similarly, the typical university student spent a wander-year visiting universities in other countries, studying under the most illustrious professors he could find, and consolidating his grasp of one or two foreign languages. Travel thus achieved a new dimension, being performed not only for essential purposes, but to improve skill and knowledge.

Other nonbusiness travel was done for health reasons. Ancient Romans traveled far to spas in Italy, Austria, and France, seeking remedies in curative water or mud for their ailments. These were only the wealthy, of course, but physicians for hundreds of years have been prescribing travel as one way of improving the health. Often doctors found that a change of air, of climate, of associations made people feel stronger. Europe's spas, which fell out of favor with American doctors as medical practice grew more "scientific" in the 20th century, are not only still in business, but are attracting more people than ever before, including the patients of American doctors.

Travel for the pure pleasure of it—tourism—has been one of the special privileges of the rich since the most ancient times. Europe's spas, in addition to being health centers, were also social centers with plenty of activity such as balls, picnics, plays, and concerts. They became more and more popular after stagecoaches were replaced by comfortable trains and sailing vessels by reliable steamships.

In America, too, there was summer travel by the rich to spas in Virginia, Pennsylvania, and Arkansas, as well as to summer estates at the seashore or in the mountains. The Grand Tour of Europe, which had become a tradition for aristocratic British students upon their graduation from Oxford or Cambridge, became a fashionable once-in-a-lifetime excursion of six months to a year for America's new industrial and mining and railroad millionaires.

Wars have always stimulated travel. The Crusades, for example, gave Europe an interest in the Middle East that lasted for centuries, with trade and business travel flourishing between military campaigns. It was World War I that really brought intercontinental travel down to prices that middle-class Americans could afford, having piqued the interest of the millions who went there to fight. Steamships were in their heyday, and the War had built up their passenger-carrying capacities.

At the same time, wide-ranging domestic travel also had come within the reach of Americans because of the proliferation of inexpensive automobiles and hard-surfaced roads. As the automobile enabled people to travel further afield, such expensive resorts as Lakewood and Cape May, New Jersey, to which the wealthy had traveled by train from nearby cities, suddenly lost most of their tourist trade. Florida and southern California became destinations for mass travel, and many people began to travel during the winter to good mountain slopes for skiing. As a result, there began a burgeoning of beach, mountain, and ski resorts.

Then came World War II. Many millions of young American men and women were sent to Britain and all over Europe, to Hawaii, Alaska, the Philippines, China, India, Australia and New Zealand, the islands of the Pacific, North Africa and the Middle East, and finally, to conquered Japan, Germany, and Italy. These young people were fascinated with what they saw and did in other lands, and, naturally, they wanted to go back.

During the war years, aviation had come into its own. After the War, aerial troop transports were converted to serve the new traveling public as passenger aircraft, giving Americans a new kind of opportunity—travel to Europe for a vacation of only two weeks. U.S. aircraft factories, with huge capacity developed during the war, converted to the manufacture of passenger planes and soon were supplying them to the new airlines that were springing up all over the world.

Travel now was possible for just about any American who wanted it—in his own car throughout most of North America, or on low-priced excursion and charter flights to other continents. Worldwide tourism increased 1,000 percent from 1950 to 1970, a phenomenal advance. To support this increase, there had to be a commensurate increase in the infrastructure that sustains tourism and attracts tourists—hotels, gambling casinos, amusement parks, marinas, airports, highways, beach facilities, ski resorts, aircraft, buses, cars, restaurants, entertainment and sports facilities, rental cars and boats, and a host of less visible items such as electricity, gas, telephone, and water supply systems in resort areas.

War-torn Germany and Japan, starting from rock bottom in 1946, worked hard and built their economies into powerful positions within 20 years. Profits filtered down, and soon German and Japanese tourists were being seen all over the world, along with Britons, French, and Italians.

Tourism requires some affluence, along with the feeling that travel is a desirable and rewarding activity. There are still about 3 billion people in the world who have neither the incentive nor the means to travel because their lives are totally occupied with the struggle for survival, including most of Black Africa and the hordes on the Indian subcontinent, for example. In the countries of the two large Communist blocs, many citizens may have the intellectual curiosity and perhaps even the means to travel, but it is forbidden, except on the business of the government or on government-sponsored projects. We tend to take travel for granted, but we should bear in mind that to the world's economically and politically depressed majority, it is an unattainable luxury.

Travel is coming to be regarded as a necessity in North America. Inflation in Europe and America, severe dollar devaluation, and an oil shortage imposed by the Arab nations reduced U.S. travel to Europe in 1974 by 10-15 percent. But Americans did not stop traveling. During the severest part of the oil shortage, people went to resorts near home, and many of these recreational areas had record years. The oil shortage eased, but unemployment and inflation worsened during the winter of 1974-75, yet Florida and other southern areas were jammed with tourists.

Dr. Louis F. Twardzik, chairman of the Department of Park and Recreation Resources at Michigan State University, said:

"The great number of tourists crowding Florida resorts this winter wasn't really an unnatural phenomenon in times of social stress. Instead, it is merely an expression of the high value people place on their recreation today. The economic picture is severe enough to trigger a higher demand for recreation by people at all economic levels."

Two points here are of importance to the person considering a career in travel. First, recreational travel, which was a luxury for the rich alone during most of the world's history, has come to be regarded as a necessity in the United States for people of the lower middle class as well as for those of the middle and upper classes. It is very broadly based. Second, if travel by certain modes or to certain destinations becomes too expensive or otherwise difficult, people will switch to other modes or destinations, but they will continue to travel for pleasure. This indicates stability for the industry as a whole, regardless of ups and downs for particular segments.

HOW BIG IS THE TRAVEL INDUSTRY?

The American Society of Travel Agents (ASTA) recently announced results of a survey showing that, for the average American family, travel-related expenditures rank second only to expenditures for groceries. Difficult as it is to believe, the total U.S. national tourist market in mid-1975 was $61 billion. Actual travel-agency sales increased from $5 billion in 1970 to $11 billion in 1974. ASTA also found that tourism is one of the top three industries in 46 states in the U.S., ranking second in many of the remaining states. In Hawaii, tourism generates more income than the main export products, sugar and pineapple. In the U.S. Virgin Islands, three-quarters of the area's total income is from tourism. Florida, California, and such other "sun spots" as the Mississippi Gulf Coast and the Texas coast depend heavily upon tourism. It may come as a surprise to learn that heavily industrialized New Jersey finds that tourism is its second most important industry. On every sunny summer day, New Jersey has more than a million people on its 128 miles of beautiful beaches.

Travel is one of the major industries of the United States, and in many countries of the world, it is by far the major industry. In coming decades, steadily increasing leisure time and earlier retirement age will make it more and more important. Beyond the fact that travel is a huge and strong industry that should afford a good degree of stability in travel-related work, it has a great intangible attraction. People in travel jobs are helping other people to go somewhere special, where they will relax and enjoy themselves. In our sedentary society, there are many who travel to find a challenge for their bodies—skiing, surfing, scuba diving, or mountain climbing.

With equal zest, others travel to find the challenges to the mind that appear in contrasting one's own feelings and actions against those of people in another country. Most groups believe they are inherently superior to others. Travelers refresh themselves in the discovery that theirs is not the only way of life, that they can learn from other cultures, that their habits and thoughts are not even acceptable to many people. They also find that they can contribute an occasional workable idea in a foreign setting.

The travel worker, whose hours are passed with travelers seeking physical and mental challenge, relaxation and change, finds constant stimulation from working with travelers and helping them to fulfill their desires. Helping others to travel stimulates one's own urge to go places, and being in the industry gives one special advantages for personal travel.

PERSONAL TRAVEL

A special inducement offered by careers in travel is the possibility of traveling oneself–at nominal cost, or totally free, or, better still, being paid to travel. Constant travel with a salary can be enjoyed as a member of a flight crew or a ship's company. Paid seasonal travel is available to tour directors–usually men and women who have worked their way up in a travel agency. Long-haul bus drivers, hostesses, and railroad train crews also are paid for constant travel.

Employees of airlines, passenger shipping lines, passenger rail lines, and bus lines, whether they travel in their jobs or not, usually are given liberal free or reduced-rate personal travel for themselves and their immediate families, beginning soon after they start working. Airline personnel, in addition to flying for little or nothing on their own airlines, usually can fly for only nominal charges on other lines as well.

Travel agency personnel are so important in bringing business to air, rail, ship, and bus companies that these carriers offer them trips at very low rates and may offer free trips to familiarize them with new routes or cruises. Operators of tourist resorts or attractions and national tourism offices of foreign countries also give free familiarization trips to travel agents and sometimes to their staffs. Very low hotel rates usually are available to travel agency personnel. State and city travel promotion bureaus, resort operators, national travel bureaus of other countries, hotels, and carriers also provide free trips for travel writers who write regularly for magazines or newspapers or who write books about travel. Additionally, employees of hotel chains, when traveling, usually can stay at their companies' hotels at a fraction of the regular rates.

Thus, people in most travel-related jobs can enjoy personal travel for themselves and their immediate families at very low rates or even at no cost. This is one of the attractions of the travel

industry, of course, and it is the reason that salaries in many travel-related jobs are lower than those for similar work in other fields. Many persons are willing to work for less than they could make at other jobs in exchange for abundant travel privileges.

OPPORTUNITIES FOR WOMEN

The field of travel is one of the best for women. Air travel, for example, developed the position of stewardess, giving women an opportunity for a glamorous position, a chance to meet all sorts of people under good conditions, and practically unlimited travel. Women are relied upon to sell tickets for airlines, trains, buses, and all kinds of attractions. They work in travel agencies, in public relations offices, and in many departments of hotels. Women are guides and lecturers in national parks, lifeguards and recreation directors at pools and beaches and parks, and they do most of the office work that must take place in connection with every enterprise in the field of travel.

More than this, however, women are moving up in the travel industry. They are becoming officers of corporations that own hotels, department managers in all sorts of resort and amusement and hotel enterprises, and many have gone out on their own to perform services independently. Among the latter are free-lance travel writers, operators of travel agencies, owners of travel attractions, and operators of guide services.

One of the highly successful women in public relations related to travel is Ms. Marguerite Allen, senior vice president of Robert F. Warner, Inc., in New York City. Her firm represents about 80 of the world's most distinguished hotels in a dozen U.S. states and twenty other countries around the globe. For these hotels,

(Left) Opportunities for women in the travel industry are increasing not only in numbers, but also in the range of positions becoming available.

the company accepts reservations at its offices in various U.S. and Canadian cities and performs many kinds of publicity and public relations functions. About opportunities for women in travel, Ms. Allen says:

> "The travel industry offers women the best of both worlds—great career opportunities and the opportunity to travel. More specifically, airlines provide jobs ranging from stewardesses to executives in the public relations field; travel agencies not only employ women on all levels, from guides to counter personnel, but many women, in fact, have become owners of their own agencies; and hotels sometimes have women managers, certainly women house-keepers, which is a highly paid job, as well as women public relations officers. It is doubtful that any woman can become wealthy in this field, but it offers a wealth of diverse interests and there is never a dull moment."

THE BROAD VARIETY OF TRAVEL JOBS

Transportation, travel, and tourism provide work for about one person in eight in the United States. With such a tremendous number of personnel, it is easy to realize that the variety of occupations within the field or closely allied to it is almost without limit. For example, a doctor, a manicurist, a chef, and a horn player all become part of the travel business if they work on a ship, or at a resort such as Walt Disney World.

The travel world, therefore, is not a single profession or vocation, but dozens of professions and occupations. Education for travel-related work, then, is of many different kinds, and there is no single way to prepare oneself for any travel job.

In the pages that follow, travel industries will be considered, one at a time, and the main career opportunities in each industry will be analyzed, their educational preparation will be discussed, and specific steps for getting started will be detailed.

CHAPTER 2

AIRLINES

Not counting military aviation, over a half million people are employed in America's aviation industry. U.S. airlines alone carry about 200 million passengers and over $1 billion worth of freight every year. Aircraft account for more than 75 percent of public intercity passenger miles traveled within the U.S. and about 95 percent to points abroad.

Pay is fairly high in the airlines, and working conditions usually are good. Since continued growth of the industry is expected, future prospects for employment are bright. It must be noted, however, that because of energy problems in the 1970s, specifically the skyrocketing cost of jet kerosene, many airlines cut out unprofitable routes or reduced service and, therefore, suspended hiring. Should the energy situation worsen, there could be reductions in service, with a consequent reduced need for new personnel. This would be temporary, however, since expanding population alone is bound to necessitate increasing air traffic. Airlines work is exciting, and the industry is still young and growing. It is a field which is attractive to adventurous young people, so if you join it, there are likely to be social rewards in working with other lively and interesting employees.

FLIGHT ATTENDANT

This position usually is referred to as *stewardess, hostess,* or *steward.* In past years, the employees who served food and drink and attended to passengers' wants on U.S. airlines had to be female, unmarried, young, attractive, and in the early days of aviation, short—because of the low ceilings in passenger crafts. At one time, airline companies also required that stewardesses be nurses.

There had been male stewards on some European airlines for many years, but most U.S. lines preferred young women because they glamorized air travel and attracted passengers. However, a young man who was refused a stewardess job by an airline sued the line, charging sexual discrimination. He was upheld by the court, and since then, the airlines have had to consider both men and women eligible for positions as flight attendants.

Other job qualifications also have changed. A woman no longer must be unmarried to be a flight attendant, but she does have to be willing to live in a city designated by the airline by which she is employed. The flight attendant should no longer be short, because aircraft ceilings are much higher than in years past. Pillows, blankets, and small luggage are stowed in overhead cabinets or racks, and attendants must be tall enough to reach them. There are some variations in most of these qualifications, so if you don't fit a certain airline's specifications, look for an airline that fits yours. Eastern Air Lines, for example, accepts stewardesses from 5'2" to 5'9" tall and stewards from 5'7" to 6'2". Trans World Airlines says flight attendants of either sex can be 5'2" to 6'2" tall. United Airlines wants flight attendants 5'2" to 6'0" in height, as does Delta Air Lines. The acceptable weight of the applicant is expressed as "in proportion to height" by most airlines, although some of them define this with a listing of the maximum weight acceptable at specific heights. Minimum age for flight attendants varies from 19 to 20 (Delta, United, TWA, PanAm, for example) to 21 (Eastern).

Most airlines require flight attendants to be high school graduates, although some, such as Eastern, say something such as, "A high school diploma or G.E.D., while not required, is preferred." In actuality, most airlines want people who have had

The position of steward or stewardess is one of the most visible and challenging travel occupations, since its primary purpose is passenger service.

two years of college, nursing training, or experience in dealing with the public. If such people are available, those with just high school graduation generally are not hired.

Eastern says, "U.S. immigration policy in most cases prevents us from considering anyone who is not a U.S. citizen or an alien with a permanent visa." This is true of all U.S. airlines. Since most foreign airlines have a policy of hiring their own nationals, it is difficult for an American to get a job with one unless he or she has some special required qualification such as fluency in several languages. Excellent English is expected by all airlines, and if you hope to work on an international route, you should have what PanAm calls "a fair background in one other language."

Vision should be good, and if it needs correction, the airlines prefer contact lenses. United, TWA, and Eastern will accept glasses, but Delta does not. Several airlines mention that if contacts are worn, they should have been used successfully for at least half a year before applying for the job. The airlines have varying requirements as to minimum visual acuity with and without correction.

General health should be excellent, including the hearing. Most airlines give flight crews regular flight physical examinations to make sure they remain in good condition and ready to cope with emergencies.

All the airlines stress the importance of good appearance. Eastern says:

"The very high visibility of a flight attendant necessitates extremely high personal appearance standards. Factors evaluated are: (1) posture and carriage (walk); (2) complexion—must be clear and well cared for. Distracting scars, moles, and blemishes may be disqualifying; (3) teeth—must be white, straight and even; (4) grooming—hair should be well groomed and smartly styled."

Delta says:

"The main qualities Delta interviewers look for in flight attendant applicants are a neat, wholesome appearance and the ability to project themselves and their personality. Airline flight attendants have a public relations as well as a service job. Their responsibility is to care for passengers on their flight in such a way that passengers will prefer Delta Air Lines over any other mode of transportation."

At PanAm:

". . . we think an airline should do more for its passengers than provide transportation and a meal. We're talking about professional assistance every step of the way. Helping passengers plan their business trips and vacations. Suggesting hotels and scheduling reservations. Making their flight as relaxing and enjoyable as possible. Providing information and assistance after they arrive. PanAm makes a lot of

promises to its passengers. And we count on our
Flight Service Crew Members to fulfill them. You'll
be representing PanAm to people from all over the
world. So you have to *enjoy* meeting them . . . talking
to them . . . and bending over backwards to make
them comfortable."

TWA wants its flight attendants to have:

". . . an attractive appearance, poise and a natural
ability to communicate, and flexibility as it relates to
job assignment . . . a mature and self-starting individual who has the ability to work well under pressure
and still maintain concern for people."

TRAINING

Specialized training for flight attendant jobs is offered by
various private schools, but generally speaking, such programs are
not likely to help get you a job. Every airline either operates its
own training facilities or sends its new flight attendants to a
school, sometimes operated by another airline, with which it has
a contract.

Training by the airlines is of four or five weeks' duration.
PanAm trains at the Miami (Florida) Training and Development
Center for four weeks, followed by about ten days of in-flight
and base training at the city where the new employee is stationed.
PanAm's curriculum covers passenger service, aircraft familiarization, crew conduct, first aid, customs regulations, currency
conversion, aircraft documentation, emergency equipment and
procedures, personal grooming, in-flight food preparation, meal
and beverage service, geography and cultures.

TWA trains its student flight attendants at Breech Training
Academy in Overland Park, Kansas. TWA's combination school

and dormitory has 300 guest rooms, with two students sharing each room.

TWA describes its training program as follows:

"During the five-week training course, your instructors are all line flight attendants capable of relating to your individual questions. In training you will become knowledgeable in the areas of safety and aircraft. You will learn about our fleet of aircraft. Aircraft mock-ups will be available to you for training purposes. In addition, you will be going on observation flights, as well as actually working on flights in order to prepare yourself for your new position. Along with the aircraft training, you will learn emergency safety procedures which will serve to develop your self-confidence in handling any emergency situation.

"After becoming proficient in aircraft and safety, you will begin classes in the service area. Instruction in this area entails everything from serving a cocktail to preparing a chateaubriand with poise and confidence.

"Throughout the training period, you will be involved in classes pertaining to corporate awareness, personal development, customer service concepts, and appearance and grooming techniques."

Delta conducts its flight attendant training school at its headquarters, Hartsfield Atlanta International Airport, in Atlanta, Georgia. Students are instructed and housed in the same building. During the four weeks of training, school is in session from 8 to 5, with plenty of study to do every evening and a midnight curfew. The three weekends are taken up with observation flights. Delta says:

"A substantial portion of the training program is devoted to physical fitness and good grooming, and the Training Center reflects this emphasis. A complete beauty parlor is part of the large make-up room where trainees learn to style their hair and to accentuate [their] best features through proper use of cosmetics. Exercise equipment is available for those who want to use it.

"The first week of study is devoted to physical examinations, uniform fittings, grooming instruction, general introductory briefings on Delta history and policy, and enough fundamental aircraft nomenclature to get the trainees through the following weeks of specialized study of each individual Delta plane.

"During the course they also learn basic flight theory—lift, gravity, thrust, and drag—and the jurisdiction and function of governmental agencies and all other agencies even remotely touching on airline operation.

"Among facilities for safety procedures is a specially equipped balcony from which trainees receive realistic training by actually operating and sliding down an emergency evacuation chute.

"To practice in-flight service, trainees use still another area, an aircraft mock-up, which contains 29 seats (21 tourist and 8 first class), fully equipped galley, public address system, panels for lighting and air conditioning, and coat closet. They practice meal service by serving each other. A successful service is quite an exciting event. It's also fun, for the trainees get to eat the meals, representative of what they will soon be serving on their own flights. They practice voice improvement and correct diction, ready for the day when they will be making flight announcements over their plane's public address system. "Instructors are Delta stewardesses who have been flying for several years. They are attractive, knowledgeable, and experienced. The curriculum is complex, but there is a very low failure rate. Graduation is a reward of the 4-week course, and smart new uniforms are trimmed with Delta wings."

WORK LOCATIONS

The home base at which a flight attendant lives most of the time is called the domicile. This is not a dormitory, but a city in which the employee has an apartment. Eastern Airlines has domiciles in Atlanta, Boston, Chicago, Miami, Newark, New York, San Juan (Puerto Rico), and Washington, DC. PanAm's bases are in New York, San Francisco, Miami, Seattle, Washington, Los Angeles, Houston, London, and Honolulu. TWA's International Flight Attendants are domiciled in New York and Los Angeles, and its Domestic Flight Attendants are based in those cities and in Chicago, Kansas City, and San Francisco. United's domiciles are in New York, Newark, Washington, Miami, Honolulu, Chicago, Denver, Los Angeles, San Francisco, and Seattle. Delta bases are in Atlanta, Boston, Chicago, Dallas, Houston, Miami, and New Orleans.

At United, "New flight attendants are assigned to fill domicile openings by preference bidding based upon chronological age. After nine months at the first domicile, they may transfer to other locations every six months." At TWA, however, "Newly graduated flight attendants are assigned to available domicile openings according to company requirements and must be willing to relocate to one of these domiciles after training. After the 5-month probationary period, you may bid to other domiciles based on flight attendant seniority."

If you want to remain permanently in the same city, try an airline with short routes—generally called *feeder* lines—where there's a good chance of your getting home to the same bed every night. On the long routes, no matter where you are domiciled, you are likely to spend several nights each month in a hotel room provided by your airline at the far end of the route.

At Delta:

> "For the first few weeks after graduation, new flight attendants are on 'reserve.' This means that instead of having regular flights, they are on standby basis and must be available on designated reserve days to fill in whenever and wherever they are needed. They are soon given the opportunity to 'bid' each month on the routes they would like to fly. Since seniority is the deciding factor, new flight attendants usually have to wait for what they consider choice assignments."

EMPLOYMENT AND SALARIES

Delta trained 713 new flight attendants in 1970, 487 in 1971, 596 in 1972, 926 in 1973, and 489 in 1974; at mid-1975, Delta employed 4,270 flight attendants. The U.S. Department of Labor reports that there were 39,000 flight attendants employed in 1972 and projects 1985 requirements at 76,000—an increase of 92.4 percent with annual openings of 8,000 every year (5,500 replacements and 2,500 new jobs).

The Federal Aviation Administration (FAA) requires one flight attendant for every 50 seats on an airliner, so as aircraft grow in size, the number of flight attendants increases. There may be only one stewardess on a small aircraft and up to 16 on a Boeing 747.

A Department of Labor survey of union contracts covering several large domestic and international airlines in 1972 showed the earnings of beginning flight attendants ranging from $600 to $665 per month, with experienced persons receiving $875 to $925 a month. PanAm's 1975 starting salary (after training) was $571 for 67 flight hours per month, plus premium pay for each hour up to 80. For example, 75 hours' work would bring $669. With periodic raises, after two years, 75 hours' work per month would bring $896.

As of April 1, 1975, when a new contract went into effect, TWA flight attendants earned base pay of $547 for 65 flight hours (international) or 68 hours (domestic), with automatic increases up to $864 after nine years' service. Overtime was paid for hours worked above the base numbers, and there was an expense allowance.

United Airlines flight attendants start, after training, with a base salary of $537 per month for the first six months, covering 65 hours of flying. Each additional hour earns $11, up to 85 hours. There are regular subsequent increases, and there is an allowance for meals, limousines, and uniform maintenance.

At Delta:

"A new flight attendant receives a salary of $700 per month for the first six months of employment. For the next six months, you receive a base rate of $605 per month for the first 50 hours of flying time. Since 80 hours is the usual maximum flying time per month, the hours flown between 50 and 80 earn pay of $10.44 per hour. You are guaranteed a minimum of $775 per month after six months, regardless of the number of hours flown. By the 10th year of service, base pay is $765, and hours over 50 are paid at $13.25 per hour."

ADVANCEMENT

Advancement from the position of flight attendant comes with seniority and merit. PanAm's pursers, who handle money that passengers pay for drinks in flight, earn up to $1,242 per month for 75 hours. The flight service director, who is in charge of the cabin crew, can earn $1,360 per month for 75 hours. Nonflying positions to which flight attendants can be promoted include jobs as instructor, customer service director, and recruiting representative. Stewardesses who are particularly beautiful, photogenic, and charming may be chosen to model for the airline's advertising photographs and can sometimes work into the line's public relations staff.

At Delta, which has historically insisted upon promotion from within, an example of promotion possibilities is provided by Ms. Norma Wildes. She joined Delta in 1959 as a stewardess and after three years of flying out of Miami and Atlanta, she became secretary to Delta's director of engineering. In 1965 she became one of five Delta female sales representatives, and within half a year became coordinator of women's services for the airline. In this position, she oversees the production of such travel information and services to women as a guide to efficient packing, recipe booklets, films showing secretaries and secretarial students how to book air reservations, and other projects to make travel by Delta appealing and easy for women.

JOB DUTIES

In addition to serving meals and drinks, flight attendants have other duties. They board the flight early to check cabin equipment, adjust lighting and ventilation, and check supplies and meals before the passengers board. They hang up passengers' coats; see that carry-on luggage is properly stowed; check seatbelts; control smoking during takeoff, landing, and turbulence; pass out magazines, pillows, and blankets; and make flight announcements. They also demonstrate emergency oxygen and flotation equipment and point out escape doors. They check passenger manifests before takeoff, direct passengers to the proper seats, and take care of flight reports, caterers' invoices, and requests for supplies or for special attention to equipment.

Flight attendants must soothe angry or frightened or sick passengers; serve drinks and meals as rapidly as possible; and take care of any special needs of passengers or the flight-deck crew. They often must work under tension, and on long trips, they may be serving dinner at midnight and breakfast two hours later. Vacation travel often starts Friday evening or Saturday morning and ends Sunday evening, so a stewardess may often find herself working in the sky instead of enjoying a Saturday-night date.

On the other hand, flight attendants generally have all the fringe benefits available in comparable office jobs. In addition, they have considerable variety in their work and the added bonus of free or very inexpensive travel.

AIRLINE PILOTS AND COPILOTS

A job whose glamour is equal to the work of the flight attendant is that of the *airline pilot*. In addition to their prestige, pilots are highly paid wage earners, earning up to $72,000 per year. This figure is rising as aircraft grow larger and more complicated.

JOB DUTIES

The pilot arrives at the airport well before takeoff time. After getting information from the meteorological office about weather conditions between where he is and where he's going, the pilot works out route, speed, and altitude in a conference with the airline dispatcher. He then coordinates this flight plan with the air traffic controllers. The copilot is generally with the pilot during these conferences and assists as requested in working out practical routes and altitudes.

They proceed to the airplane, where they check the controls, engines, and instruments, going down a long checklist item by item. Passengers board and are strapped in; the cabin-crew chief advises the pilot that they are ready; and the pilot obtains permission from air traffic control to taxi and then to take off. Once airborne and on course, frequent radio reports are made to controllers on the ground en route as to the plane's altitude, speed, and position, the weather, the amount of fuel remaining, and anything unusual about the flight. Altitude and speed are changed, also the plane's heading, as the pilot deems necessary. Instruments detailing the condition of the engines, the amount of fuel in each tank, the altitude, airspeed, and other factors are constantly scrutinized.

In case of an emergency, such as an engine's becoming too hot or ice forming on the wings faster than it can be melted, the captain must take time, distance, fuel, and other factors into consideration. If he shuts down one engine, for example, it will take him longer to reach his destination.

If low fog or clouds obscure the field at the destination, an approach on instruments may be necessary, with a controller on the ground "talking the plane down." Leaving the aircraft after the flight, the pilot and copilot must fill out records of the flight at the airline office before they have completed their day's work.

Some senior pilots become instructors. There is a considerable need for them, because every time an airline starts using a new model of airplane, the line's pilots must be given instructions on how to fly it. Sometimes the first airline to start using a new model will instruct the pilots of several other airlines.

Airline pilots must operate at peak efficiency for long periods of time, but their efforts usually are well-rewarded in job benefits and salary.

The FAA requires that each pilot's performance be evaluated at least twice each year. Senior pilots take specialized training to become evaluators so they can check out other pilots.

Not all pilots in the travel trade fly large passenger planes. Some of them are *bush pilots* who still "fly by the seat of their pants" to wilderness lakes, perhaps carrying a couple of fishermen whose canoe is lashed to the undercarriage of the floatplane. Skiers are borne to the tops of otherwise inaccessible mountains by helicopter pilots, so they can ski down over miles of virgin snow. Single-engine aircraft tow gliders up 3,000 or 4,000 feet above ground level and release them to soar in the empyrean. Sport parachutists are taken aloft, a little planeload at a time, then they jump out and aim for ground targets.

There are also many very small airlines, operating a small number of one- or two-engine planes to island resorts, offshore gambling havens, camps in the woods, and other places where there is a continuous but small stream of travelers. As an example, a small-plane airline in Las Vegas flies tourists on a sightseeing trip up the Grand Canyon, lands them on the rim for a ground tour, and flies them back to Las Vegas in the sunset. In such an operation, the pilot may conduct the ground tour, pick up the passengers from their hotels, and perform his own aircraft maintenance. He has considerable independence when airborne, but much less support from the ground than has the pilot of a commercial airline.

REQUIREMENTS

Safe flying is the major ability demanded by airlines of their pilots. Punctuality for on-time departures and arrivals also is desirable, but safety is always paramount. Heroes are really not desired in this job. Airlines prefer steady, eminently well-qualified persons who take pride in the perfectionism of the detail with which they check out equipment, weather, and all the many items that might possibly go wrong and cause trouble in flight. In addition to being a perfectionist, a pilot must be cool in emergencies. His flying experience, often in the military, will probably have subjected him to many emergencies, perhaps in combat, where his mettle was tested and proved.

The actual minute-by-minute supervision of the aircraft in flight is not much work nowadays. Whereas early pilots sometimes navigated by following highways and were lost when they got into fog, the modern pilot has all the advantages of radar and loran, radiocompass, and many other helpful instruments. In addition, his flight is monitored from the ground by flight controllers who can advise him of his precise position and warn him about weather difficulties ahead, other aircraft in his path, or about dangerously low altitude.

The pilot of past years controlled his course constantly with a joystick; however, modern aircraft are flown mechanically during most of a flight, except during takeoff and landing. On most long flights, a minor compass correction once or twice an hour is about all that is needed to keep the aircraft in straight and level flight and on the shortest course to its destination. A computer makes all the tiny corrections that used to be made by a pilot's sensitive fingers on the joystick. But the pilot, the copilot, and usually the flight engineer must be able to take control and fly the aircraft in any sort of emergency that might develop—from minor turbulence to losing an engine to diving the plane down to safe altitude if the cabin is ruptured and depressurized.

From this, you can see that most of the pilot's skill and ability are almost never used, but are held in reserve in case of need. For individuals who want continual challenge to which they can respond vigorously, this kind of work can be frustrating and stultifying. An airline pilot does not have the exciting outdoor fight against fate and the elements that Charles Lindbergh had in his open cockpit plane. Instead, he spends long sedentary hours just keeping an eye on things.

At the beginning and end of every flight, however, the pilot earns his high pay, as he lifts his monstrous machine into the air and brings it safely back to earth. The pilot often is called the *captain* by the airlines. Like the captain of a ship, he has total responsibility for the safety of passengers, crew, and cargo. In the air, all passengers, as well as the flight crew, are subject to his orders. The copilot often is called *first officer* by the airlines, and the flight engineer *second officer.*

Many licenses are required for airline pilots and copilots. The FAA administers a rigid flight physical for the commercial pilot's license to persons at least 18 years old with a minimum of 200 hours of flight time. Then a written test is given on FAA regulations, navigation in the air, flight safety, and other subjects. Finally, pilots are given a flying test, with an examiner aboard the plane.

This license is qualified so that the pilot is permitted to fly only single-engine, multi-engine, or floatplanes. It is further qualified for the particular types of aircraft in which the pilot has been checked out, such as Lockheed 1011 or Boeing 747.

An airline transport pilot's license is required for airline captains. To get this, you must have an instrument rating, which requires flying under instrument conditions for 40 hours or more. You must be at least 23 years of age, with 1,500 hours or more of flight time in the previous eight years.

The commercial license is valid as long as the flier can pass the annual physical and semiannual flight evaluation, but no pilot is permitted to fly an airliner after he reaches 60. At or before this age, many pilots are transferred to ground duties, usually in operations.

The airlines publish minimum requirements, but all of them add something such as this advice by Eastern:

> "Because of the large number of extremely well-qualified pilots currently available for the few positions which exist throughout the industry, the competition has been quite intense. The majority of candidates seeking employment possess a bachelor's degree, plus have jet or turbo-prop training and experience. Typically, they have well in excess of 1,500 total flight hours."

Delta strongly suggests getting a bachelor's degree, then joining the Air Force, Navy, Marines, or Army for flight training: "A great majority of Delta's pilots receive their flight training in military service."

This is true throughout the airline industry. Learning to fly in a civilian flying school is possible, but costly, and it could be difficult acquiring the 1,500 hours of flight time required for the transport license. In time of war, when the military is using all the pilots it can get, the airline industry would no doubt take new pilots with minimum qualifications or even less than minimum. But just after a war, when there are thousands of pilots looking for flying jobs, the airlines can take their pick, and they naturally choose the most highly qualified.

PanAm's basic qualifications are: age 20-31; height 5'6"-6'4"; vision 20/20 uncorrected; minimum of two years of college or equivalent; FAA commercial license and instrument rating; FAA first class medical certificate; FCC (Federal Communications Commission) third class radiotelephone operator's license; minimum 500 hours single or multi-engine; U.S. citizen or resident on an immigrant's visa capable of getting a passport.

PanAm says that any of the following qualifications would improve your chances of becoming a pilot: college degree; FAA airline transport rating; FAA flight engineer's license: FAA navigator's license; military training and experience; aeronautical, mechanical, or electrical engineering background.

Eastern's minimum qualifications are: age 21 years; a bachelor's degree from an accredited college; FAA commercial pilot's license with instrument rating and restricted radiotelephone operator permit; fixed-wing flying time varies in relation to other qualifications, but 1,500 hours desired; first class FAA medical certificate, including 20/20 uncorrected vision in both eyes; height 5'6"-6'4".

At Delta, the minimum requirements are: age 21; 5'8" height; weight in proportion to height; college degree preferred; first class physical; FAA instrument rating; FAA commercial license; FCC restricted radiotelephone license; fixed-wing multi-engine flight experience preferred.

Very few people are hired to start as pilot (or captain) for the major airlines. Most begin as flight engineers, with eventual promotion to first officer and finally to captain. Reaction time and ability to make rapid correct judgments under stress are tested, and cockpit crewmembers must maintain excellent physical condition to keep their jobs.

TRAINING AND SALARIES

Before he takes up passengers, the newly hired flight engineer, copilot, or pilot is given extensive training by the airline. This includes classroom instruction in meteorology, FAA regulations, company policies and rules, and other facets of general orientation. He may also be given three to ten weeks of flight instruction consisting of lectures, time in simulated aircraft, and actual flights. A new trainee who does not have a rating for the type of airplane he will be flying must earn it.

New Delta pilots have eight weeks of ground training in Atlanta, followed by 30 to 45 days of flight training. Eastern trains for 5 to 15 weeks in Miami. PanAm says:

> "If you are selected as a pilot with PanAm, you will report for training immediately to one of PanAm's training centers in New York, Miami, or San Francisco. (Probationary period as a pilot is usually one year.)
>
> "Once at PanAm's training schools, all students receive five weeks of instruction in company orientation, federal aviation regulations, dispatch procedures, intensive aircraft familiarization, and systems operation. Pilots assigned navigation duties receive an additional 10 weeks of specialized navigation training, while pilots assigned flight engineer duties receive an additional eight weeks of aircraft system instruction and flight-engineer flight training. All new pilots receive four weeks of initial flight training in the type of aircraft to which they will be assigned and recurrent training each six months thereafter."

Domiciles for Eastern cockpit crews are in Atlanta, Boston, Chicago, Miami, New York, and Washington. PanAm bases its pilots in New York, Miami, Houston, Seattle, San Francisco, Los Angeles, and Berlin. Delta pilots are based at Atlanta, Chicago, Boston, Dallas, Houston, Miami, and New Orleans.

Starting pay for pilots with the airlines is not particularly high, but it rises steadily with seniority. The Department of Labor reports that as of 1970, pilots and copilots averaged $17,026 per year. Airline pilots and copilots earn more than those employed by corporations or government. Most airline pilots are members of a union, the Air Line Pilots Association, International. Some belong to another union, the Allied Pilots Association. Pilot pay is decided upon by bargaining between union and company.

One union contract in 1972 showed copilots earning from $17,500 to $40,000 per year, while pilots were paid from $37,000 to $60,000 per year. The Air Transport Association, national organization of the scheduled airlines, announced 1975 salaries for copilots as ranging from $8,000 to $42,000 per year, and for pilots, $30,000 to $72,000. Pay in the senior brackets has thus been rising very rapidly.

As to initial salaries, Delta pays $650 per month during training; $700 during the first six months of work; and $725 for the next six months. This ends the probationary period, after which pilots bid on bases and routes with variable rates of pay.

Simulated aircraft flying is only part of the multi-faceted training necessary to become an airline pilot.

COURIER-JOURNAL & LOUISVILLE TIMES

Eastern pays $650 per month from the time training starts; $700 during the second six months; then the second-year pay averages $1,100 or more.

PanAm starts probationary copilots at $600 per month for six months; $800 for the rest of the first year. "As a B-707 jet copilot on increment pay during your second year, you will receive $998 per month (minimum guarantee) or $1,228 for 80 hours, and during your third year $1,237 per month (minimum guarantee) or $1,522 for 80 hours."

Pay varies with the type, size, and speed of the airliner, as well as with the number of miles and hours flown. Guaranteed minimum pay is about four-fifths of the maximum pilots could earn. They are paid extra for international and night flights.

Work schedules are irregular, since they are based on when the majority of people want to fly. Vacationers typically want to fly on weekends and during nonbusiness hours. Airline pilots, on average, are away from home bases overnight about one-third of the time or more. Airlines provide them hotel rooms and expense allowances for this.

The Federal Aviation Act forbids airline pilots and copilots to fly more than 85 hours per month. Most of them fly about 60 hours, but total hours on duty, including layover time before return flights, usually rise to over 100.

Most pilots and copilots enjoy liberal vacations and other fringe benefits, including a considerable amount of free or low-cost personal travel. Joining an airline's cockpit crew is difficult and keeping the job is challenging, but the responsibility, pay, and prestige make it well worthwhile.

The Department of Labor reports that 52,000 pilots were employed in 1972, about half of them as commercial airline pilots and the rest as pilots of corporation jets, aviation instructors, air taxi pilots, crop dusters, etc. The projected requirement for 1985 is 78,000—a growth of 43.8 percent over 13 years. Annual openings for 2,000 pilots are expected, consisting of 500 replacements and 1,500 new jobs. As with other jobs in the airline industry, these figures will be altered by the relative scarcity or abundance of fuel and its price, as well as by the price of airline tickets and the general state of the economy.

FLIGHT ENGINEERS

Whereas the *flight engineer* is low man on the cockpit crew, as noted in the section on pilots and copilots, he is a top man in the industry on mechanics, engine overhaul, and electronics of the aircraft. His job combines the fields of operations and maintenance of the aircraft. He is expected to be able to take over as captain of the plane if the pilot and copilot should in some way become unable to act. He eventually is promoted to copilot and then to pilot.

JOB DUTIES

The main practical operating responsibility of the flight engineer, however, is to know every blade and bolt and valve, every sparkplug, transistor, wire, pipe, and tank on his aircraft. His place in the cockpit is well supplied with instruments which report on every critical point and phase of engine operation, electronic systems, fuel and its flow, temperature, and many other conditions.

When any instrument or combination of instruments shows something unusual, the flight engineer must be able to diagnose trouble rapidly, report it immediately to the pilot, and, if possible, repair it in flight or arrange for removal of stress from an affected part until mechanics on the ground can repair it. If the next stop is at a small airport without mechanics trained for his type of aircraft, the flight engineer may repair it himself.

On a typical flight, the flight engineer joins the pilot and copilot in the preflight weather briefing and conference on route and altitude. Together they check the aircraft's maintenance record to be sure that needed overhauls and equipment replacement have been made as required. Arriving at the airplane, they inspect the exterior briefly, including the tires.

The flight engineer assists the pilot and copilot in making preflight checks of equipment, controls, and instruments in the cockpit, and he checks fuel levels, electric power, and engine-report instruments. In flight, he adjusts controls to keep the engines at maximum efficiency and records engine performance and fuel consumption at frequent intervals. He watches cabin pressure and temperature and adjusts them as necessary.

PERSONAL REQUIREMENTS AND TRAINING

The same physical and height and weight standards are required by the airlines for flight engineers as for pilots and copilots—and the same coolness under fire. A high school education is required, and some airlines require some college as well.

The best way for flight engineers to obtain the necessary training is in the armed forces, just as for pilots and copilots. An FAA flight engineer's license is required. Qualification for this consists of three or more years' experience as a pilot or flight engineer in the armed forces, or in repair and overhaul of aircraft engines. A stiff flight physical examination and a written test on engine operation and the theory of flight also are required for this license, plus a flight check in an aircraft of the type to which the engineer seeks assignment. An applicant without armed services experience can study for the license at a private aviation school

(Right) Pilot, copilot, and flight engineer are dependent on each other for vital information concerning the aircraft's route, altitude, and mechanical condition.

DELTA AIRLINES

approved by the FAA. Also required is the commercial pilot's license, described in the section on pilots and copilots.

EMPLOYMENT AND SALARIES

According to the Department of Labor, about 7,000 flight engineers were employed in the U.S. in 1972. This number is expected to expand by 35.7 percent to 9,500 in 1985. Average annual openings are expected to number 300, of which 200 will be new jobs and 100 replacements.

The earnings of flight engineers started at about $650 to $690 per month in 1972, rising to $24,000 to $36,000 per year. In 1975, the range was $8,000 to $37,000. Not all flight engineers are qualified as pilots, but those who are belong to the Air Line Pilots Association, International. Most others belong to the Flight Engineers' International Association or the International Brotherhood of Teamsters, Chauffeurs, Warehousemen and Helpers of America.

AIRCRAFT MECHANICS

This occupation is taken up here chiefly because it is one way in which a young person can prepare himself to become a flight engineer. There are more than twice as many *aircraft mechanics* as there are pilots, copilots, and flight engineers combined. Although the mechanics are seldom seen by the traveling public, there would be no flying without them.

There are three main specialties among aircraft mechanics: powerplant, airframe, and instrument mechanics. In addition to doing such routine preventive maintenance as changing engine oil, greasing wheel bearings, and replacing sparkplugs, aircraft mechanics dismantle engines, check all the parts for wear, and rebuild them. The FAA requires regular inspection of airframes and power plants, and it is the aircraft mechanics who do the inspections. When a flight is delayed for emergency repairs, mechanics must work fast to get the plane back into the air.

EMPLOYMENT AND TRAINING

Of the 123,000 aircraft mechanics employed in 1972, over 40 percent worked for the airlines, 25 percent were in aircraft manufacture, 20 percent worked for the federal government, and most of the rest worked in small independent repair shops. More than half of all airline mechanics work at airports near New York, Miami, Chicago, Los Angeles, San Francisco, and Dallas. An airline usually operates a major repair base for each type of aircraft in its system.

Training for most mechanics consists of graduation from high school or vocational school, plus some experience in a machine shop or auto repair shop. Major airlines operate apprenticeship programs of three or four years' duration, combining classroom and on-the-job training. A person who has been an aircraft mechanic in the armed forces can complete his apprenticeship rapidly, or if he is fortunate enough to have worked with aircraft very similar to those the airline flies, he might step right into a mechanic's job. The FAA has a list of mechanic schools which it has approved, and they will make the list available to anyone who is interested. Programs at most of these schools are of one and a half to two years' duration.

Graduates of these schools, or mechanics with 18 months of experience, are eligible to take the written and practical tests for a license either as an airframe or power plant mechanic. A mechanic trying for both licenses at once must have 30 months' experience. Airframe mechanics are qualified to work on wings, fuselages, and landing gear, while power plant mechanics work on engines.

Licensed mechanics advance with increasing seniority and ability to lead. A mechanic may become a crew chief, inspector, shop foreman, maintenance supervisor, and perhaps, company executive. Some start their own shops and work on contract for small airlines, corporations, government agencies, or other general aviation aircraft operators. Others learn to fly well enough to earn a commercial pilot's license and become flight engineers.

The general employment outlook for aircraft mechanics is good, since continued expansion of all phases of aviation is expected. There may be temporary setbacks in the field because of fuel shortages or economic slumps, but a 53 percent increase in jobs is expected by 1985, with the total rising to 190,000.

Starting pay for mechanic trainees in 1972 was $4.19 per hour, rising to $6.55 with experience, as agreed to in union contracts—most airline mechanics are unionized. Pay for qualified airframe and power plant mechanics in 1975 was $12,000 to $15,000 per year on the scheduled airlines. Additionally, free or low-cost travel on their own and other airlines, plus other generally good vacation and fringe benefits, are standard for mechanics with major airlines.

Unions representing aircraft mechanics include the International Association of Machinists and Aerospace Workers, the Transport Workers Union of America, and the International Brotherhood of Teamsters, Chauffeurs, Warehousemen and Helpers of America.

FLIGHT DISPATCHERS

No airliner is permitted to take off until the company's *flight dispatcher* gives permission, so this is a position of great responsibility. With information at hand on the status of the airplane, the crew, the weather at his own airport and all around the destination airport, the dispatcher confers with the flight crew and decides on the best route and altitude for the flight, alternate routes and destinations in case of deteriorating weather, and all other flight details.

If the flight should have to be canceled because of equipment breakdown or a blizzard, for example, the dispatcher must see that the passengers and crew are advised. Some dispatchers must keep records of aircraft and equipment status and availability, cargo weight for each flight, hours flown by each aircraft to assure overhauls in time as required by the FAA, and flying time of all flight crews so they do not exceed FAA monthly maximums.

TRAINING AND EMPLOYMENT

There are many ways to prepare for a position as dispatcher. At least two years of college is helpful, and a bachelor's degree in mathematics, physics, or perhaps meteorology is preferred. Experience in business, in flying, or in meteorology also helps. Airlines and private schools also give courses approved by the FAA, and radio operators, ground dispatch clerks, and air traffic controllers can work up to jobs as flight dispatchers. A job as assistant dispatcher does not require FAA approval, but to be a flight dispatcher, one must earn the FAA dispatcher certificate.

After any of the several combinations of work or study mentioned above, or military dispatch work, an applicant may take the dispatcher's test. A written examination covers airport and airway traffic procedures, meteorological analysis, facilities for air navigation, radio procedures, FAA regulations, and other subjects. An oral examination tests a candidate's familiarity with navigational facilities, airways, and weather maps.

Airlines give their dispatchers training in any new flight procedures and in the capabilities and limitations of new aircraft, and the dispatchers are tested regularly. The dispatcher must know exactly how much each aircraft can carry as well as its

cruising and landing speeds. If a plane must make an emergency landing just after takeoff, the dispatcher must be able to compute quickly how much fuel it must dump to get down to safe landing weight and speed.

Dispatchers are a select group—there were only 800 of them in 1972. Their numbers are expected to stay about the same through 1985, with openings for only about 20 replacements per year. The main reason for the lack of growth in this special job is the improvement in communications. Dispatchers in central locations are expected to be able, with the help of computers and advanced communications, to dispatch aircraft from faraway fields.

Flight dispatchers were earning $14,500 to $22,000 in 1975. They receive free and inexpensive travel as airline employees and liberal vacations and fringe benefits. Most belong to one of two unions: the International Association of Machinists and Aerospace Workers, or the Transport Workers Union of America.

TICKET AGENTS, RESERVATION AGENTS, AND CLERKS

Reservation agents and *clerks* for major airlines generally work in large numbers in central offices. As the human link between the telephone and a computer terminal, the agent gives information on flight schedules and the availability of seats and makes reservations. Agents receive calls from the general public, from travel agents, and from their company's ticket agents. They generally do not come face-to-face with inquirers, but do all their contact work by telephone.

Ticket agents work at ticket counters in airports and in central-city ticket offices. They answer questions about fares and

(Left) Ticket and reservation agents have a vast storehouse of information at their fingertips—becoming the human link between computer-stored information and the passenger.

schedules, give out timetables and descriptive literature, check with reservation agents for seat availability, and sell tickets. Fares are so complicated in air travel that selling a ticket is a more difficult procedure than it might seem. Ticket agents check in baggage, add any excess-weight charges, and issue boarding passes to permit passengers to get to the airplanes.

Ticket agents, being in direct contact with the public, are as smartly uniformed as flight crews. They are selected on the basis of pleasing personality and appearance, good diction, and education. High school graduation generally is required, and two or more years of college preferred. Chances for advancement are improved by college courses in traffic management and other phases of transportation.

The loading of baggage and cargo is supervised by *operations* or *station* or *ramp agents,* and sometimes even performed by them. They see that cargo weight is evenly distributed in the aircraft and keep cargo manifests and lists of numbers of passengers. They may also announce arrivals and departures.

Outside salesmen for the airlines often are called *traffic representatives.* They visit shippers and corporations, keeping present customers happy and trying to obtain new customers. Ticket and reservation agents may advance to supervisor in these specialties or to traffic representative.

Heading all sales efforts are *city sales managers,* and above them, *district sales managers.* The district sales manager administers ticket and reservations offices, directs the efforts of sales representatives, and promotes and develops traffic on his airline.

In 1972, beginning reservation, ticket, station, and operations agents earned from $600 to $700 per month. In 1975, the Air Transport Association (ATA) quoted salaries as follows: *ramp agent*—$8,500 to $13,000; *sales representative*—$12,000 to $18,000; *district sales manager*—$18,000 to $30,000. Other office jobs performed in the airlines earned the following salaries in 1975, as quoted by ATA: *personnel representative*—

$12,000-$19,000; *research analyst*—$12,000-$19,000; *programmer*—$12,000-$18,000; *accountant*—$12,000-$18,000; *business-machine operator*—$7,000 to $10,500; *teletypist*—$7,000-$10,500; *switchboard operator*—$6,000 to $9,500; *secretary*—$7,000 to $12,000; *stenographer*—$6,000 to $9,500; *typist*—$5,500 to $9,000; *file clerk*—$5,500 to $9,000.

AIR TRAFFIC CONTROLLERS

The U.S. Federal Aviation Administration is the employer of 20,000 *air traffic controllers*. Most are stationed at major airports or at airways traffic control centers near large cities. A few work outside the United States.

The importance of the air traffic controller cannot be overstated, for he must manage all air traffic—often in the face of weather changes, runway hazards, or overburdened airports.

CHRISTIAN SCIENCE MONITOR NEWS & PHOTO SERVICE

The semidarkness of the control tower is where the controller performs his essential work as guardian of the airways. He radios permission to pilots to taxi, take off, or land. He must simultaneously keep track of many aircraft that may be on the ground or in the air, and he must know the characteristics and speed of each type of aircraft, so he can utilize the often overloaded airstrips as efficiently and safely as possible. He uses various electronic devices to locate aircraft, communicate with them, and guide them down to a safe landing.

After an airliner takes off, the airport controller "passes" it to a route controller who is responsible for the first segment of its trip. The route controller has radar and other electronic gear to keep the aircraft in "sight" even though it may be flying at 35,000 feet and in the dark. He warns the pilot about any weather changes, aircraft near his course, or other hazards and helps him as necessary to remain on course.

The route controller passes the aircraft to the next controller on the airway, and there may be a succession of them, so that an airliner flying on a prescribed air route is almost always in contact with the controller. The last route controller on the trip passes the aircraft to the controller in the tower of the destination airfield for instructions to join a holding pattern or to land and taxi to the debarkation point.

Heavy responsibility puts air traffic controllers under great stress, so anyone entering this kind of work should be prepared to cope with extremes of tension over long hours. Unlike other U.S. Civil Service employees, controllers may retire on pension after only 20 years of work—a recognition of the wear and tear they undergo.

TRAINING AND EMPLOYMENT

Applicants for controller duties must be under 31 and have vision correctable to 20/20 and clear, precise diction. They should be college graduates or have three years of progressively more responsible work experience demonstrating ability to learn and perform air controller duties—or both. Competitive examinations are given by the Civil Service System.

Chosen applicants are given classroom and on-the-job training to learn aircraft performance characteristics, aviation regulations, the airways system, and controller equipment. At the FAA Academy in Oklahoma City, intensive training in flight simulators is given. Full qualification as a controller takes two to three years. Every controller is examined physically once a year; twice a year he is examined on his job performance. Controllers can advance to *chief controller, regional controller,* and to administrative positions in the FAA.

Control towers never close down, so controllers must work frequent night shifts on a rotating basis. In addition to their 40-hour work week, they may work extra hours for overtime pay or compensatory time off. The government gives them 13 to 26 paid vacation days and 13 days of sick leave annually; life and health insurance; and a salary of $14,000 to $19,700 per year. Controllers are represented by the Professional Air Controllers Organization, and their salaries are determined by collective bargaining and spelled out in contracts.

CHAPTER 3

SHIPPING LINES

The U.S. Merchant Marine has been in sad straits for years because of the cost of American labor, both for building ships and for manning them. This cost is three or four times as high as shipowners in Europe and Asia must pay. As a consequence, U.S. shipping has been surviving only when heavily subsidized by the government, or when heavy defense spending for military or aid ventures brought employment to U.S. ships.

Congress in 1970 agreed to subsidize the construction of 30 new ships per year until 1980. This vigorous construction program was intended to revitalize U.S. shipping, but in actual practice, older ships are being retired or scrapped at the same rate new ones are being built.

Many U.S. shipping companies have registered their ships in Panama, Liberia, and other countries in order to pay low taxes and avoid high labor rates. Americans can work on these ships, but at low rates of pay. Also, having worked on a ship flying a "flag of convenience," an American may have a difficult time eventually working on an American-flag ship, because a U.S. union might refuse him membership.

Passenger transportation across the oceans has been falling off rapidly in competition with airlines, and most of the great passenger liners have been retired or adapted to the cruise trade. Cruising has been gaining in popularity and appears to be the salvation of the passenger ship. Fly-cruise packages, in which a vacationer flies to Miami or Port Everglades in Florida, or to a Caribbean port, have become more and more popular. New York City, from which about 100 cruises go south every winter, opened a brand-new passenger-ship terminal at the end of 1974 to increase its cruise business. Cruises up the inland waterway to Alaska, and from West Coast ports to South America and the Caribbean also are increasing their sailings and bookings.

Careers at sea are still possible for Americans, on U.S. or foreign-flag ships, and even in the U.S. passenger trade. The Department of Labor reports that there were about 8,500 officers and 23,500 seamen working on U.S. oceangoing ships in late 1972. Of these, about 64 percent were aboard freighters; 32 percent aboard tankers; and the remaining 4 percent aboard passenger ships.

Shipboard work is divided among three departments. The *deck department* operates and navigates the ship, maintains the hull and deck equipment, and supervises loading, storing, and unloading of cargo. The *engine department* operates and maintains the propulsive machinery. The *steward's department* feeds the crew

As transoceanic passenger ships have lost popularity, cruises have gained rapidly—offering a gracious and slower-paced form of travel.

COURIER-JOURNAL & LOUSIVILLE TIMES

and passengers and cleans the living spaces.

It is possible to become *captain* of a ship with no formal education. The catch is that there are many Coast Guard examinations to take along the way in order to qualify for the various licenses that are necessary to advance. The person with no educational background is up against exceedingly severe competition from graduates of the one federal and five state merchant marine academies.

Doing it the hard way, a young person would obtain seaman's papers from the Coast Guard; wait in a union hiring hall until shipped out as an ordinary seaman; after a year take examinations to become an able seaman; after three years at sea take examinations for third mate; and at annual intervals, take examinations for second mate and master status. However, this progression would take many years, and even with master's papers, the seaman might not become captain of a ship.

The better path to advancement is attendance at the U.S. Merchant Marine Academy at Kings Point, New York. Like the service academies, entrance is by congressional appointment and College Entrance Board examinations. Students are paid a small allowance, and their education is free. The second year is spent at sea aboard a U.S. commercial ship. Each graduate receives a bachelor of science degree, a license as third mate or third assistant engineer, and an ensign's commission in the U.S. Naval Reserve.

The Merchant Marine Academy usually places all its graduates in seagoing jobs before they graduate. A Merchant Marine officer's career from this point depends upon his doing a good job, studying for examinations for second mate and master, and taking them as early as possible. After this, he simply must work and wait until he makes captain.

Engineer officers have similar careers, gradually working up to chief engineer. The five state academies are: California Maritime

Academy at Vallejo; Maine Maritime Academy at Castine; Massachusetts Maritime Academy at Hyannis; Texas Maritime Academy at Galveston; and New York Maritime College at Fort Schuyler, New York City. All these schools charge tuition.

People in the steward's department generally work up from such unskilled jobs as messman and utilityman to third cook, second cook (the ship's baker), and chief cook. Above the chief cook is the chief steward. He is not a ship's officer, but nevertheless is answerable only to the captain. On a passenger ship, the steward's department is by far the largest, employing many waiters and room stewards.

Opportunities for women exist on passenger ships, as stenographers, typists, and secretaries; as hostesses; as beauticians and manicurists; as cashiers and assistant pursers; and as cruise directresses. Women often entertain aboard cruise ships as singers or dancers. There is often a registered nurse aboard a large passenger ship, who may function as the surgeon's assistant.

Shipboard personnel receive free room and board, so they are able to save most of their earnings, if they wish to do so. Base pay per month on a freighter in 1972 was: *able seaman*—$528; *ordinary seaman*—$413; *messman*—$410; *chief steward*—$694. Premium rates are paid for overtime. Officers generally can earn about 50 percent above base pay for overtime and extra responsibilities. Some 1972 basic rates: *third mate* and *third assistant engineer*—$858; *first mate* and *first assistant engineer*—$1,347; *chief engineer*—$2,253; *captain*—$2,443. There are numerous strong unions covering most seafaring jobs.

Further general information on merchant marine officer and seaman jobs is available from:

> Office of Maritime Manpower
> Maritime Administration
> U.S. Department of Commerce
> Washington, DC 20235

Information on job openings, wage scales, and employment prospects may be obtained from the nearest union office or from the applicable union's headquarters:

International Organization
of Masters, Mates and Pilots
39 Broadway
New York, NY 10006

National Marine Engineers'
Beneficial Association
17 Battery Place
New York, NY 10004

National Maritime Union of
America
346 West 17th Street
New York, NY 10011

Seafarers' International Union
of North America
675 Fourth Avenue
Brooklyn, NY 11232

CHAPTER 4

RAILROADS

After World War II, the airlines gradually took over most of the long-haul domestic passenger traffic which traditionally had belonged to the railroads. Service on many lines became so poor that it seemed the railroads were trying to get rid of passengers. As new population centers developed, there were many places not served by rail, and no new rail lines were laid. Intercity bus service improved and carried most of those passengers who did not fly or use their own cars.

By 1970, railroads were accounting for only one percent of intercity passenger miles. In order to preserve some rail service, the federal government in 1971 created Amtrak, the National Railroad Passenger Corporation. ("Amtrak" is a contraction of "American track.") Amtrak started operating with only 150 intercity trains, a far cry from the 20,000 in service in 1929.

Amtrak was started just in time. It finally had been admitted that automobiles were a prime cause of air pollution, and that all civilized countries were going to have to reduce individual transportation by improving mass transportation, which causes less pollution. Then came the energy crisis of the winter of 1973-74, which jolted Americans into the realization that a really severe shortage of gasoline could *force* the use of mass transit.

There were many growing pains, as Amtrak strove to meet rapidly increasing demands. New types of trains were designed and built, many cars were bought, and a nationwide computerized ticketing and reservation system was installed and operating

in 1974. Many of the roadbeds were in poor repair, and introduction of high-speed trains would have been pointless until the roadbeds were improved. Amtrak improved the New York-Washington trackage so the fast Metroliners could travel at 110 miles per hour, and they planned similar improvement on 12 other main routes. Stations, equipment, repair facilities, and maintenance shops belonging to the original railroads are being taken over gradually by Amtrak and are being upgraded.

From the point of view of the person considering a career with a railroad, it is important to note that Amtrak gradually is taking over more and more employees from the original railroads and adding them to their own payroll. So far, Amtrak has taken over all station personnel dealing with passengers and all the service personnel aboard the trains—this includes the cooks, porters, waiters, and car attendants, but not the conductors, engineers, firemen, and trainmen. Amtrak also operates its own reservations and marketing operation. In June 1974, Amtrak had 8,800 employees. This still is only a small fraction of all the people working for the railroads. The Department of Labor noted 575,000 railroaders working in 1972, making this one of the country's largest industries. In this chapter, we shall consider only jobs on the trains and working with passengers—the *travel* jobs of railroading.

PASSENGER SERVICE REPRESENTATIVE

A new railroading occupation introduced by Amtrak is the *passenger service representative* (PSR). The PSRs are personable young men and women who are much like airline flight

(Left) Railroad stations, many of which have become architectural landmarks in their own right, have been idle in recent years; but convenience and energy considerations are attracting travelers once again to rail transportation.

Railroad reservation and information clerks, like their counterparts in the airline industry, work from a vast bank of computerized information to make reservations and answer passenger inquiries.

attendants, but who have different duties. They help passengers and see that their needs are satisfied, and they are trained in railroading so they can answer most questions passengers ask.

Additionally, the PSR files a detailed report after every train trip, specifying whether or not the train was on time, describing passenger service and the operation of the equipment, and presenting any passenger suggestions. In this way, the PSR functions to show the train-riding public that Amtrak is interested in riders' viewpoints so that the company can act to improve its service.

Unfortunately, Amtrak was hit by the economic recession of 1974-75, and one of its economy moves was to trim down the PSR program to only a few long-haul trains. It was hoped that this program would be expanded. In their bright red and blue uniforms, the PSRs bring to the railroads some of the glamour and vitality that flight attendants confer upon the airlines.

RESERVATION AND INFORMATION CLERKS

Amtrak's nationwide computerized reservations system is also an innovation in passenger railroadings. *Reservation* and *information clerks* work around the clock to give schedule and fare information and take reservations for Amtrak trains. These clerks work with telephone, computer-readout console, and computer terminal at five major locations: Bensalem, Pennsylvania; New York City; Chicago; Los Angeles; and Jacksonville, Florida. Other clerks at central-city ticket offices and at railroad stations may consult computer-readout consoles and may quickly enter reservations. Toll-free telephone numbers connect the general public with the clerks at the reservations centers, who can handle up to 65,000 calls per day.

The conductor is in charge of the train—collecting tickets and money, signalling when to start or when to make emergency stops, and supervising freight transfers.

COURIER-JOURNAL & LOUISVILLE TIMES

CONDUCTORS

The conductor is in charge of the train, whether it carries freight or passengers. He signals the engineer when to start, and he can order a stop for any emergency. *Passenger-train conductors* collect tickets and money and furnish schedule and fare information. *Freight-car conductors* maintain records of the freight in each car and its destination and make sure that cars are dropped off or added to the train as their cargo dictates.

Conductors are almost all male and are promoted from the job of *brakeman,* which also is called *trainman.* Passenger-service brakemen attend to car lighting and temperature and may help collect tickets. Passenger brakemen and conductors earn an average of $1,190 and $1,337 per month, respectively. Conductors, brakemen, and all train-crew personnel may work irregular hours, including nights and weekends—they get premium pay for overtime. Most brakemen and conductors belong to the United Transportation Union.

ENGINEERS AND FIREMEN

Locomotive engineers drive great machines powered by diesel engines or electricity. There were 35,000 of them in 1972, and those in passenger service averaged earnings of $1,540 per month. A few are hired and trained to become engineers, and a few are promoted from brakeman positions after examinations. Most, however, are promoted from fireman. There is no fire to feed in diesel locomotives, so the fireman is really an assistant engineer. Newly hired firemen should be between the ages of 21 and 35, with a high school education and excellent hearing, eyesight, and color vision.

The new fireman is trained on the job by the engineers with whom he rides and is given a regular assignment when one is available. Within a year of being hired, he starts an engineer training course of six months, composed of both formal instruction and on-the-job training. He must pass numerous tests to qualify as an engineer, then may have to wait several years until there is a vacancy. Firemen in passenger service in 1972 earned an average of $1,292 per month.

Most engineers and some firemen belong to the Brotherhood of Locomotive Engineers. Some engineers and many firemen are members of the United Transportation Union.

STATION AGENTS

Station agents in small stations sell tickets, check baggage, compute express and freight charges, and may direct the operation of some trains. In progressively larger stations, the station agent is a supervisor of these activities or an administrator of a large staff. Station agents usually are promoted from the ranks of railroad clerks, telegraphers, telephoners, and towermen. Those in the last three groups direct the movement of trains from towers in terminals and yards. To be hired, they should be high school graduates and have excellent hearing, eyesight, color vision, and diction.

CLERKS

Clerks are the largest group of railroad employees. They work in railroad stations, company offices, yards, terminals, and freight houses; there were about 83,000 of them in 1972. Most railroads require a high school education and may require applicants to take a clerical aptitude test. Some clerical training or experience also is beneficial. Most clerks belong to the Brotherhood of

Railway, Airline and Steamship Clerks, Freight Handlers, Express and Station Employees.

Railroad clerks can advance in many directions—to cashier, executive secretary, accountant, statistician, chief clerk, auditor, ticket agent, station agent, buyer, or supervisor.

WAGE SCHEDULE

JOB CATEGORY	START	6 MOS.	12 MOS.	18 MOS.
Accounting Clerk	35.94	37.10	38.25	40.56
Baggageman	35.94	37.10	38.25	40.56
Clerk-Steno	35.94	37.10	38.25	40.56
Clerk-Typist I	35.09	36.21	37.34	39.59
Clerk-Typist II	33.49	34.56	35.62	37.76
Clerk-Commissary	36.31	37.47	38.64	42.00
Commissary Worker	34.29	35.39	36.48	38.69
Computer Operator	39.34	40.61	41.89	44.43
Consumer Correspondent	35.94	37.10	38.25	40.56
Crew Assignment Clerk	39.34	40.61	41.89	45.00
Duplicating Machine Operator	35.94	37.10	38.25	40.56
Information Clerk	35.09	36.21	37.34	39.59
Janitor	31.77	32.79	33.80	35.83
Key Punch Operator	35.09	36.21	37.34	39.59
Material Control Clerk	34.29	35.39	36.48	38.69
MTST Operator	35.94	37.10	38.25	40.56
Junior Clerk	31.77	32.79	33.80	35.83
Rate Quotation Clerk	39.34	40.61	41.89	44.43
Receptionist	33.49	34.56	35.62	37.76
Red Cap	31.77	32.79	33.80	35.83
Reservation & Information Clerk	36.31	37.47	38.64	40.97
Secretary I	38.40	39.63	40.87	43.35
Secretary II	37.41	38.62	39.82	42.23
Secretary	35.94	37.10	38.25	40.56
Staff Assistant to Regl. Mgrs.	39.34	40.61	41.89	45.00
Station Laborer	33.49	34.56	35.62	37.76
Statistical Clerk	35.94	37.10	38.25	40.56
Telephone Switchboard Operator	35.09	36.21	37.34	39.59
Ticket Accounting Clerk	39.34	40.61	41.89	45.00
Ticket Clerk	39.34	40.61	41.89	45.00
Timekeeper	38.40	39.63	40.87	43.35
Travel Clerk	39.34	40.61	41.89	45.00
Usher/Gateman	33.49	34.56	35.62	37.76

SALARIES AND EMPLOYMENT BENEFITS

Reproduced above is the wage schedule which became effective August 1, 1974, resulting from the agreement between the Brotherhood of Railway, Airline, and Steamship Clerks, Freight Handlers, Express and Station Employees and Amtrak. The wages shown are for one day of eight hours or less. Overtime earns premium pay.

Amtrak wants its employees to advance and has a program to provide educational assistance for employees who want to take job-related courses of study. There is also a very liberal pass policy at Amtrak and on most nonpassenger railroad lines. Amtrak employees have *unlimited* free transportation on a space-available basis, excluding certain special high-fare trains. Employees' spouses and dependents are given 12 free trips a year and as many more as they desire at half fare.

More information on salaries, job openings, and job specifications is available from any specific railroad for whom you may want to work or from any of the thirteen unions with which Amtrak has bargaining agreements. You may wish to write directly to:

> Amtrak
> 955 L'Enfant Plaza North S.W.
> Washington, DC 20024

Or to:

> Association of American Railroads
> 1920 L Street N.W.
> Washington, DC 20036.

CHAPTER 5

BUS LINES

The United States had 3,786,713 miles of public roads and streets in late 1974, of which 36,021 miles were in the magnificent Interstate Highway System. What a change has taken place since stagecoaches on rudimentary trails were replaced by intercity buses! The first such bus route was established in Oregon, between Bend and Shaniko, in 1905. Early buses, without springs and riding on solid tires, were exceedingly uncomfortable and often broke down. Drivers had to be innovative mechanics, but even with their best efforts, a bus sometimes had to be towed home by a borrowed team of horses.

With all today's miles of excellent roads, buses can go almost anywhere in the United States, including large areas not served by airlines or trains. As efforts are strengthened to reduce dependence on private cars in order to reduce both pollution of the air and fuel expenditure, the use of buses will be increased vastly.

The modern intercity bus provides not only transportation, but also large windows and sometimes an upper deck for viewing the scenery. Most also offer air conditioning, restrooms, and comfortable reclining seats, in addition to a high degree of reliability in meeting schedules and an exceedingly low accident rate. Buses used especially for sightseeing may also have kitchens like those on aircraft and hostesses who serve meals. They also may have tour guides who point out interesting sights in passing and lead the passengers when they disembark to visit a particular site.

Thus, buses are an important segment of the travel scene and will be growing even more important. There are more than 20,000 intercity buses in the United States, most of which are controlled by one of the two major nationwide intercity bus operators—Greyhound Lines, Inc. and Continental Trailways.

Greyhound Lines is a single corporation. It started in 1914 with a two-mile run for 15 cents in an open seven-passenger car, from Hibbing to Alice, Minnesota. Continental Trailways is a combination of a large number of companies, many of them managed independently.

Another major bus operator in the travel field is Gray Line Sight-Seeing Companies Associated, Inc. In the United States, Gray Line has a total of about 8,000 employees in its various companies; about 3,000 of these are drivers, of whom some ten percent or more are women.

Gray Line companies operate both long-distance and local sightseeing tours. The *drivers* also serve as tour guides, so they have to be familiar with the sights on the route as well as being capable drivers. They also are expected to have good diction and a pleasant manner. They are well compensated, earning an average of over $15,000 per year as they conduct Gray Line's 1,140 tours.

Of the total 8,000 employees working for Gray Line, there are some 1,100 *reservation and information clerks,* who are constantly in touch with the traveling public and travel agents by telephone or in person.

Inquiries about jobs with a Gray Line company should be made to one of its 153 member companies around the world.

DRIVERS

Long-distance bus drivers start the day's assignment with a thorough check of their buses—brakes, steering, wipers and

The well-developed interstate highways in the U.S. have made possible an extensive system of bus lines.

blades, lights, mirrors, fuel, oil, water, tire pressure and condition, fire extinguisher, first-aid kit, emergency reflector. They obtain tickets, change, and report forms as required.

Driving from the garage or terminal to the bus station's loading platform, the driver parks, then collects tickets or money as passengers board. Over a public address system, he announces the destination, time of arrival, and stops en route. The driver regulates the lights and temperature and does what he can about any passenger complaints. He also may load or supervise the loading of suitcases and express packages.

If he can, the driver repairs any malfunction occurring on the trip, such as changing a flat tire. On arrival, he makes out a report on the distance traveled, times of departure and arrival, fares collected, and any mechanical difficulties or accidents on the bus. The U.S. Department of Transportation requires him to keep a log of hours worked, and any fines incurred for speeding or reckless driving must be paid by the driver himself.

EMPLOYMENT AND TRAINING

The Department of Labor reports that there are over 25,000 intercity bus drivers, whose average annual earnings are over $12,500. Salaries are computed at an average of 19.7 to 22.8 cents per mile driven, although an hourly rate is applied for short runs. Driving schedules average less than 39 hours per week, ranging from six to ten hours per day, three to six days per week. The Department of Transportation limits a day's driving to ten hours, which must be followed by eight hours off.

The Department of Transportation has minimum age, health, and experience standards for intercity bus drivers, but company standards are generally higher. Continental Trailways, which employs 4,000 operators, requires high school graduation, age 25 or over, a high degree of driving skill, and ability to communicate

The bus driver, in addition to being responsible for the safety of his passenger and vehicle, also must handle tickets, supervise loading, answer passenger complaints, and troubleshoot mechanical problems.
CONTINENTAL TRAILWAYS

with the public. Eyesight must be 20/20 or correctable to 20/20 with glasses. Stability of temperament and emotions is important in this job, since drivers may be subjected to tension from driving long hours in traffic and from dealing with an occasional irate passenger. Continued courtesy to passengers under such conditions is difficult but important.

Newly hired drivers are schooled for 2 to 13 weeks in company policies, federal, state, and local laws pertaining to vehicle operation, timetables, price schedules, recordkeeping, minor bus repair, safety, and actual driving. They are given written and driving examinations, and the new driver must have a commercial driver's license. After that, he starts driving on passenger routes under supervision.

Although he may be completely qualified, past the probationary period, and fully approved by his company, the new driver may spend up to ten or twelve years as a substitute, filling in for drivers who are sick or on vacation, or taking extra runs, before he is assigned to a regular route.

With seniority, the driver obtains more choice assignments, which are usually the best paying ones. A few drivers are promoted to become dispatchers, supervisors, or terminal managers.

Intercity bus drivers receive paid vacations, holidays off, expense allowances or accommodations for overnights away from home, and other benefits. The independence of the job is an advantage in the eyes of most drivers, along with the opportunity to deal directly with many people in many places. Bus driving requires weekend and holiday work, however, and a driver assigned to a chartered bus on a long tour may be away from home for a relatively long period of time. A new driver may remain on call at all hours and on short notice for years before he is assigned to regular runs on a fixed schedule.

Unions representing intercity drivers are the Amalgamated Transit Union, the Brotherhood of Railroad Trainmen, and the

Some bus lines hire stewardesses—positions which often lead to opportunities as tour representatives, ticket agents, and information clerks.

International Brotherhood of Teamsters, Chauffeurs, Warehousemen and Helpers of America. Over 17,000 Greyhound employees are represented by the Amalgamated Council of Greyhound Divisions.

OTHER JOBS

Attractive young women are hired by Continental Trailways to serve as *hostesses* on their long-haul buses. The minimum age for this occupation is 18, and applicants should be good at meeting and helping people. Regarding job availability and advancement, Continental says: "Openings are usually available since many hostesses move up to other positions such as tour representatives, ticket agents, and information clerks."

Information clerks at Continental Trailways usually work in large terminals, either as telephone information clerks or information desk clerks. They should have good telephone manners and should be able to read schedules accurately. Clerks can advance to such positions as ticket agent, tour representative, or an administrative post.

Ticket agents must be high school graduates, responsible in handling money, and, preferably, sales-minded. *Tour representatives,* Continental Trailways says,

> ". . . must have a high school diploma and be able to meet the public. In addition, they should have a knowledge of world geography and be willing to travel, since they may be called upon to escort tours. The company employs thousands of representatives in this fast-growing field and offers the tour representative the opportunity to work with many modes of transportation."

Many a young person eager to become a driver, but not eligible to apply until he reaches 25, obtains a job for a bus company as a *mechanic.* Continental Trailways says, "Since the company performs all its own maintenance from rebuilding engines to upholstering bus seats, there are always openings for skilled mechanics."

Dispatchers are often former drivers or mechanics with long experience. They keep records of drivers and buses and send them to terminals or other pickup points on time.

Related jobs, if there should be no bus-line opening when you need it, include local bus driving, taxi driving, and long-distance truck driving. More and more women are becoming taxi drivers. Long-distance trucking has become a huge industry, with 570,000 drivers employed in 1972, averaging $15,800 in annual earnings.

More information about careers with bus lines may be obtained from:

Greyhound Lines Inc.
Greyhound Tower
Phoenix, Arizona 85077

Continental Trailways
1500 Jackson Street
Dallas, Texas

Gray Line Sight-Seeing
  Companies Associated, Inc.
7 West 51st Street
New York, N.Y. 10019

National Association of Motor
  Bus Owners
1025 Connecticut Avenue
Washington, DC 20036

CHAPTER 6

HOTELS, MOTELS, AND RESORTS

Throughout all history, whenever it was safe to travel, there have been places of public accommodation. In Asia and Asia Minor today, there are small inns called khans that provide only shelter. The Bible mentions that the sons of Jacob, returning from Egypt, stopped at such an inn and fed their animals. It was a khan in Bethlehem where Joseph and Mary found no room and had to go to the stables where Christ was born. Out on the roads, usually at wells, caravanserais were built at regular intervals. These can still be seen, in Turkey particularly. They are huge stone forts, large enough to hold one or several caravans with all their animals and strong enough to defend them against attack by brigands.

Ancient Persia built luxurious inns along its fine road system, as did ancient Rome. When the Romans conquered Britain, they introduced the *taberna* for drinking and the *caupona* for overnight accommodations. During the Dark Ages, travel was possible only by groups that could defend themselves like small armies. The Knights Hospitalers built many hospices for Crusaders and pilgrims to the Holy Land in the 12th century, and in western Europe from this time on, abbeys often served as inns—some still do. In England, there were about 6,000 inns along

(Left) The classic art of innkeeping has long been respected as a challenging and diverse occupation. A talent for managing a people-to-people business still must underlie an industry which has grown to gigantic proportions.

the highroads and coach routes in the 1500s. Caravanserais had been spaced about 8 miles apart, and English inns were 15 miles apart, showing that a day's journey now covered twice as much space. The Industrial Revolution and railroads caused construction of large city hotels, and spa resorts soon followed.

The first known hotel in North America was the Jamestown Inn, built the year the colonists arrived in Virginia, 1607. A postal service commenced in 1710, after which inns multiplied along the post roads. Resort hotels began opening at Eastern U.S. health spas in the 1700s, and on the seashore in the 1800s. Large hotels were built around city railroad stations, and as pioneers pushed westward, a hotel was often the first building in a new settlement.

The automobile caused construction of the first "tourist cabins" that later developed into motels. Travel increased with automobiles and later with aircraft, and hotels proliferated around the world. Several international airlines built hotels in distant, exotic places in order to provide lodging for their passengers.

By 1975, the lodging industry in the United States was earning $8.7 billion per year and employing 800,000 people. There were 21,000 hotels and 43,500 motels and motor hotels, with a total of 2.7 million rooms. Bricks and mortar provide only part of what the weary traveler wants—most of the remainder is service, which means people working to supply his wants. Out of every dollar taken in by hotels and motels, 33.1 cents is spent for employees' wages and the cost of their meals.

About half of the 800,000 hotel employees in the U.S. are women. In past years, not many women were in the very top echelons of hotel management; however, recent years have seen more and more women assuming positions of responsibility with major hotel companies. As of this writing, for example, women are in charge of public relations at the Hilton International chain, the Kahala Hilton in Honolulu, the Pacific division of Americana

Hotels, The Greenbrier in West Virginia, the Inter-Continental Hotels chain, North American operations of Club Méditerranee, Commonwealth Holiday Inns of Canada, Island Holidays Resorts in Hawaii, InterIsland Resorts in Hawaii, the Olympic in Seattle, and at The Plaza in New York. Hotel work has increasing opportunities for racial minorities in the upper echelons, too—the director of personnel at The Plaza is a Black woman, and many hotels' housekeeping departments are headed by women. In addition, women in sales, purchasing, credit, and accounting are finding no bar to continuing advancement in the hotel industry.

There are opportunities for many kinds of people in hotels. The new arrival from another country, who may have no education and may be unable to speak English, can get a job as a dishwasher or busboy. As he learns the language and the business, he can work up to a more responsible position. A girl can start as a maid or cleaner and do the same thing. One such person, John Christoforon, was hired at The Plaza in New York when he arrived from Greece, aged 15, in 1913. He worked his way up from helper, managed the employee cafeteria from 1925 until 1968, then became head cafeteria attendant when a new cafeteria was built. In 1975, he was still enjoying his job, in his 64th year at The Plaza.

Advancement is likely to be faster and further for those who enter the hotel business with an education. There are usually openings at several different entry levels in hotels, with opportunities to advance in various parts of the business.

About 10 percent of U.S. hotels are *residential*—renting or leasing their rooms for long periods. The majority of motels and hotels are in the *transient* or *commercial* category. The number of *resort* hotels is growing rapidly as more people flock to them for vacations. Many resort hotels used to be open only one season each year—employees might work in a resort in the Catskill Mountains north of New York in summer, and in a Florida hotel in winter. Now, however, northern summer hotels are using skiing

Front-office, reservation, and information clerks make initial contact with guests and, throughout their stay, are instrumental in overseeing a pleasant visit.

and other sports to attract a winter clientele, and Florida hotels stay open all year, reducing their rates during the summer.

Many a hotel or motel worker advances by saving money until he can buy his own business. Of the 110,000 managers at work in 1972, 40,000 were self-employed. There are many quite small hotels and motels, and a number of these are completely operated by family teams.

HOTEL AND MOTEL JOBS

Modern hotels offer much more than rooms and meals for travelers. The variety of services they provide adds to the number and types of hotel jobs. Besides its guest rooms and restaurants, a hotel may have special bars or nightclubs, banquet facilities, meeting rooms with audiovisual and translation equipment, large ballrooms, salesmen's exhibit rooms, swimming pools, marinas, golf courses, tennis courts, ski tows and lifts, travel agencies, beauty and barber shops, valet service, airline offices, theater ticket agencies, newsstands, gift shops, babysitting service, car and boat and plane rental, health clubs, stage and film theaters, and any other facility or service that will add income.

A large hotel may have six major departments and some auxiliary ones. The *executive* department may include a general manager, resident manager, controllers or accountants, management trainees, and directors of sales, personnel, rooms, food and beverages, housekeeping, and public relations.

In the *front office* are mail clerks, room clerks, reservation clerks, and the front-office manager. The accounting department has auditors, bookkeepers, office-machine operators, cashiers, and other clerical workers.

The *housekeeping* department includes the housekeeper, housekeeper's assistants, chambermaids, housemen who do heavy cleaning, seamstresses, decorators, upholsterers, and others. Bellmen, bellwomen, elevator operators, and doormen work under the superintendent of service in the *service* department.

The *restaurant* department has chefs, cooks of various grades and types, kitchen helpers, the steward and his staff, pantrymen, storeroom employees, dishwashers, waiters, bartenders, busboys, and other food and beverage service workers.

The *maintenance* department has stationary engineers to operate machinery for heating and air-conditioning rooms and for cooling large refrigerators. This department also employs electricians, plumbers, carpenters, painters, and locksmiths. Auxiliary departments have may laundry workers, barbers, valets, tailors, and others.

Front-office clerks do much of the hotel's minute-by-minute business with guests. The room clerks rent rooms and greet guests, assign rooms, sell various services, open billing records for new guests, advise housekeepers of arrivals and departures, and

Food preparation is a major activity within the lodging industry; many guests judge the quality of their accommodations by the quality of food service.

keep reservations lists. When a room is assigned, the desk clerk turns the key over to the bellman who takes the guest and his baggage to the room.

Reservation clerks receive reservations in person or by mail, telephone, or teletype and acknowledge them. They type out registration forms and advise room clerks of each day's list of arriving guests. They may also make reservations for a guest at other hotels on his future itinerary.

Mail and information clerks place mail, messages, and keys in guests' boxes and give these out when called for. They answer telephones and route incoming calls to the right rooms. They also may sell stamps and advise guests about transportation, attractions, and events.

The *front-office manager* supervises all these functions, coordinates the actions of the front office with those of the housekeeper and others, schedules work shifts and assignments of his clerks, inspects rooms periodically, and handles all the many kinds of complaints and problems that can arise in a hotel. Most front offices never close, at least in larger establishments, so the manager must find substitutes if his clerks fail to arrive, or fill in himself.

Some of the more elegant hotels have an *assistant manager*—often a personable young woman or man who can speak several languages. The assistant manager works at a desk in the lobby, handling non-routine matters so the front office can concentrate on renting rooms and dispensing keys and mail.

Cashiers keep track of clients' charges, total them when a guest leaves, or at regular intervals, and accept payment by cash, check, or credit card. *Accountants* bill guests regularly, handle the hotel's payroll, and prepare regular profit-and-loss statements.

For the person who is ambitious for success in the hotel business, the front office is the place to learn all about hotels and to learn to cope with all the problems that can arise. Openings for beginners' clerical jobs in the front office sometimes are filled by inexperienced newcomers, or bellmen or bellwomen, switchboard operators, or other employees who appear capable are promoted to such jobs.

EDUCATION AND TRAINING

Educational requirements for front-office jobs vary according to the type of hotel, its location, and its own standards. It is desirable to have a high school education, certainly. Graduates of 2- or 4-year colleges often start as management trainees, rotating from one department to another, but obtaining major experience in the front office. Even better for such a career is graduation from a 2- or 4-year course in hotel and motel management. These specialized curricula are becoming widespread, as colleges realize the growing importance of the lodging industry. (See Appendix B for a listing of schools offering curricula in hotel and motel administration.)

It is still possible for a person without a high school education, but with good personality and native ability and intelligence, to rise to the top in the lodging business. But such advancement becomes more difficult as college-trained people enter the business as management trainees and qualify fairly quickly for responsible work in management. So it makes sense to obtain the best education you can. In addition to more rapid advancement, the person with greater education generally can claim higher pay in top-management positions.

If you desire to enter the lodging business after a high school education, try to attend a technical high school offering hotel-related courses. Courses which might be beneficial include food service and cooking, business administration, management, and economics.

For its employees who have little or no education, the hotel industry provides training courses. In New York City, for example, the Hotel Association, in cooperation with the Hotel and Motel Trades Council, AFL-CIO, operates its Industry Training Program. Free 15-week courses, combining classroom and on-the-job training, are given at various hours to accommodate people on different shifts. Courses include English, basic accounting, repairs and maintenance, food and beverage control, floor housekeeping, telephone switchboard operation, night auditing, business machine operation, typing, and front-office procedure. Many hotel workers who started as maids or busboys have profited by these courses to become housekeepers, cashiers, auditors, and room clerks. There are similar programs in many cities.

High schools in many cities have adult education programs with specific courses for hotel workers. Some large hotels and chains have their own in-house schools, combining formal classes with on-the-job training.

The breadth of the lodging industry has grown considerably—now accommodating banquets, meetings, exhibits, sporting events, and other entertainment functions.

An industry educational program applicable to a variety of situations is that of the Educational Institute of the American Hotel & Motel Association. These courses can be taken by mail on an individual basis, in small groups without an instructor, in larger groups with instructors, or in cooperating colleges which teach Institute courses. Courses cover many topics, from the basics of sanitation and bookkeeping on up to marketing and hotel/motel property management. A single course in a special-interest subject can be taken, such as food and beverage operations, or the hotel workers can take ten courses and earn the Institute's diploma. Beyond this, by taking five courses in advanced management, having five years of industry experience, and demonstrating service to the industry, a hotel worker can earn distinction as a certified hotel administrator.

EMPLOYMENT AND SALARIES

Employment at hotels, motels, and resorts has advantages and disadvantages. There is always room for advancement for the hard worker who is willing to study and learn. When he reaches the top in a small operation, he generally can move to a larger one and keep advancing. Work in the lodging industry offers variety. A person with a good record usually can find work in any part of the traveled world, and certainly in any part of the United States. Hotel workers in a chain usually can visit in the chain's various properties at a fraction of the regular fee.

Wages are low in such jobs as busboy and maid, but job security is good, and meals and uniforms often are provided, so that the cost of living is reduced. At the middle-management level, salaries are good compared to those in other industries, and at top management levels, the salaries can be very high. Hours worked per week are comparable with those in other industries, but many jobs must be performed at night, on Sundays, and on holidays, which can disrupt social or family life.

Hourly wage rates in 1975, as shown in union contracts in 20 cities, had the following ranges: bartender from $2.32 in Miami to $4.33 in Minneapolis; bellman from $1.15 in Cleveland to $2.26 in Pittsburgh; busboy from $1.41 in Miami to $2.94 in Pittsburgh; fry cook from $2.83 in St. Louis to $3.75 in Pittsburgh; second cook from $3.06 in St. Louis to $4.33 in Minneapolis; dishwasher from $1.98 in Miami to $3.22 in Pittsburgh; elevator operator from $2.15 in Miami to $2.71 in Minneapolis; houseman from $2.25 in Cleveland to $3.32 in Pittsburgh; laundry worker from $2.09 in Miami to $2.65 in Kansas City; maid from $1.99 in Miami to $3.24 in Pittsburgh; telephone operator from $2.23 in Miami to $3.29 in Pittsburgh; waitress from $1.18 in New Orleans to $2.41 in Pittsburgh.

An industry survey of management positions in 1975 showed annual salaries being paid in the following ranges: hotel general manager from $18,000 to $36,000; hotel resident manager from $11,750 to $19,000 and up to $24,400 with companies paying a bonus; hotel food and beverage manager from $7,700 to $27,284; hotel restaurant manager from $8,633 to $12,210; hotel front-office manager from $6,676 to $14,667; hotel controller from $9.825 to $22,333; executive housekeeper from $6,432 to $16,193; hotel executive chef from $7,393 to $23,077; hotel chief engineer from $10,265 to $20,033; sales manager from $8,820 to $26,250.

SOME THOUGHTS ABOUT THE HOTEL BUSINESS

Harry Mullikin is president of a major chain, Western International Hotels, based in Seattle, and he also is president of the American Hotel and Motel Association. He assembled the following thoughts specifically for you—the young reader who may be considering a career in the lodging industry:

"The hotel industry provides an exciting, challenging career opportunity for a number of reasons. The art of hotel management as a career is one of the most challenging in the business world. An underlying factor is that it is almost completely dependent upon 'people taking care of people.'

"A successful hotel is one in which the public enjoys the experience provided by the people working in the hotel. In almost no other career can an individual meet, talk with, service, solve problems for, and provide hospitality to so many travelers. Ours is a 'people' business. People make the difference between superior hotels and mediocre ones.

"As a supervisor or department manager in a hotel, the greatest challenge is to motivate the employees to react with genuine concern, friendliness and professionalism to the guests who provide our employment. For example; to get a hotel laundry worker to fold the hand towels correctly, and to want to do it well, is a rewarding task. Employees want to do a good job, and they need to be encouraged to do so. Developing people to their fullest potential is completely satisfying. If you could do everything in a hotel yourself, it would always be just the way you wanted it. The fact that you can't, and have to trust others to deal with your guests, provides the real interest in a career in the hotel industry. The goal is to satisfy the guest. The means is by working with and through people to reach that goal.

"Another important factor of interest in a career in the hospitality industry is that there is no technical education required for success. I began my career as an elevator operator at the age of fourteen, and I now head a company with more than fifty hotels in over thirteen countries around the world. Eddie Carlson rose to President of United Airlines after starting business as a page boy in a hotel. Many of the hotel executives I know came through the ranks and obtained their positions in management because they could work with people.

"In the hotel or motel business everyone has a chance for a worthwhile life with both interest and challenge. No particular educational requirement is made for employment in a hotel, although there are some valuable courses offered which help. The quality most needed in a career in hospitality is the willingness to deal with people, both the guests and the employees.

"The future of the hotel and motel business is very bright indeed. In all parts of the world, people are traveling more and have more leisure time. People are becoming increasingly interested in visiting new places. Many hotel and motel operating companies are growing rapidly, which furnishes ever-expanding opportunities for advancement for their employees. Innkeeping is, and will continue to be, a rapidly opening field of endeavor."

Further information on hotel careers may be obtained from hotels near you and from:

American Hotel & Motel Association
888 Seventh Avenue
New York, NY 10019

EUROPEAN Travel Market

Let's go places and do things...

CHAPTER 7

TRAVEL AGENCIES

Ticket agencies have been known since ancient Rome, when postal employees sold tickets for the use of chariots and roads and made out an *itinerarium*—the ancestor of the modern traveler's itinerary. Operators of packet-boats, stagecoaches, trams, railways, and steamships sold tickets in their offices for rides on their equipment.

The business of the general travel agency, selling tickets and tours on the facilities of other companies, was started in England by a printer, Thomas Cook. Railroads had just commenced operation, and Cook, an ardent non-drinker, wanted to use them to advance the temperance cause. In 1844, he chartered a train to carry people from Loughborough to Leicester, where they would attend a temperance convention and return. Charging 25 cents each, he crowded 541 people aboard this first special train, on the first round-trip ticket in history.

Cook operated other temperance tours that were very popular. He soon realized that people were more attracted by travel at low prices than by temperance, so he began operating tours for entertainment, education, and other purposes. Ten years after his first tour, 165,000 people used his transportation and lodging arrangements to visit a great fair at the Crystal Palace in London. Cook opened a London office in 1865, by which time he was already sending tours to Europe and the Holy Land. In 1866, he led the first escorted American pleasure tour, visiting New York, Washington, Richmond, Civil War battlefields, Mammoth Cave,

Cincinnati, Niagara Falls, Toronto, and Montreal. In 1872, he led a tour of 22 people around the world. His son, John M. Cook, promoted the firm in America and other places outside Britain. In 1874, Cook introduced *circular notes* which, in a slightly different form, became known as travelers' checks, which now are issued by Cook's, American Express, and many banks.

American Express, another major travel agency, was established in 1850 by merger of the firms of Henry Wells and William G. Fargo, who also organized Wells Fargo two years later. Initially, American Express was a shipping concern, but it moved into banking and tourist services and by 1918, was out of the freight business.

Cook's, American Express, and a number of other large agencies organize and operate their own tours, as well as sell tickets for all kinds of travel. They also make individual travel arrangements, and some agencies specialize in certain national destinations to which they send frequent charter tours. Others arrange trips for youth groups, ski enthusiasts, and other particular interest groups.

However, most travel agencies do not organize tours themselves, rather, they are in the business of selling trips and tours offered by travel wholesalers and carriers. There are some 10,000 travel agencies in the United States, in 1,800 communities. Some of these are operated by the owner alone; however, the average agency has five or six full-time and two part-time employees.

The *travel agent* gives out a tremendous amount of advice and information to prospective travelers, but he makes no money unless he sells tickets and hotel reservations. Working for a travel agency, therefore, means selling, so a person not interested in selling should not enter the agency business. There are benefits to the travel agent's job—free or inexpensive "familiarization" trips by carriers and hotels, but the new employee is not likely to receive these. Low-cost air travel and hotel rooms usually are made available after a probationary period, but for the first few years, an agency employee might be able to use these only on his annual one- or two-week vacation.

Travel-agency employees need to be able to find specific information rapidly on all kinds of schedules, fares, special excursions, tour offerings, car rentals, guide services, seasonally varying hotel rates, and a host of other details. It usually takes a few months for a new employee to become really useful in an agency, especially a small agency. In a vast concern like American Express, jobs are compartmented and easier to learn.

JOB DUTIES

What does an employee of a travel agency do? Quite a variety of tasks. She or he—the majority of travel agency clerks are women—gives out travel literature about destinations, about airline and cruise "packages" that cover almost all costs for transportation and accommodations and meals, about bus tours in the local area, and perhaps helicopter and train tours. She answers questions about comparative costs for accommodations and transportation, as prospective travelers seek the least expensive or most luxurious vacations. She makes out itineraries which can be quite long and complicated if there are numerous stops and various hotels. When the client has approved a proposed itinerary, the *agency clerk* has to issue tickets and vouchers, sending copies to airlines and hotels to confirm reservations made by telephone or cable or by mail.

One of the requirements for most agency jobs is typing ability, because the agent has many forms to fill out. It is essential that these be legible to people in other countries who barely understand English. Advancing in the travel agency business, the clerk must write many letters about arrangements with carriers and about lodgings and other services.

Travel agency personnel sell travelers' checks and such special tickets as Eurailpasses on European railroads; they also arrange for rental cars and escorted tours. By agreement with other travel agencies around the world, they can offer all kinds of local services in any city the traveler might reach.

Business in a travel agency changes from month to month, according to current attractions and time and money available to travelers. School and business vacations determine when many people take trips. The rich and the retired go south in winter, and the energetic go skiing. Resort areas have high seasons and low seasons, and are always trying to extend the high season a little longer with special attractions. Atlantic City's "Miss America" contest was designed to add one week to the short summer season, for example, and it has been successful at this for over half a century. Many places have notable annual events, such as Carnival in Rio, Mardi Gras in New Orleans, New Year's Eve in Times Square in New York, and Oktoberfest in Bavaria. For the quadrennial Olympic Games, most of the accommodations may be booked as much as a year in advance.

Thus, the requests to an agency are changing constantly, and clerks must remain alert to new group tours, excursions, special fare offerings, and constantly changing regular fares and schedules.

A large part of the agent's business is arranging travel and accommodations for business travelers. This, in fact, constituted the greater part of the travel business until, in the 1970s, tourism became larger in gross billings than business travel. Some large corporations have their own in-house travel personnel to make direct bookings with carriers and for accommodations.

EDUCATION AND TRAINING

Qualification to work in a travel agency varies widely from one office to another, and some agencies will accept people without a high school education. All however, certainly prefer applicants who have completed high school. College training, of course, enables one to move up faster and further. Beginners often start out as clerks, typists, stenographers, telephone operators, or office-machine operators. As they do the paperwork, they gradually learn about the business and begin to answer inquiries and deal with the public.

For the student who hopes to enter a travel agency upon graduation from high school, valuable experience can be accumulated as a part-time employee working one or two hours per day, on Saturdays, or during summer vacations.

For the new employee in a travel agency, there are courses which help him learn the business much faster than he could by accumulated experience alone. The American Society of Travel Agents (ASTA) provides a 15-lesson correspondence course, the cost of which is reduced if the student is a member of or employed by a member of ASTA. The lesson topics are:

- *What is a Travel Agency?*
- *Travel and Geography* (Eastern Hemisphere)
- *Travel and Geography* (Western Hemisphere)
- *Domestic Air*
- *International Air*
- *Steamship*
- *Hotels*
- *Railroads and Motorcoaches*
- *Car Hire and Purchase*
- *Domestic Tours*
- *Foreign Tours*
- *Group Travel*
- *Documents and Other Services*
- *Selling*
- *Final Exam.*

In addition to this correspondence course, ASTA regularly operates a classroom course in New York City on *Travel*

Counseling & Agency Skills. This meets two evenings each week for 12 weeks, for a total of 54 hours of instruction time, with outside assignments designed to take four hours per week. The course subjects are the same as those listed above, but this course is on a more intensive and professional level.

The carrier and hotel industries also provide courses to help travel agents and their employees to serve their industries well. As an example, the Air Traffic Conference of America (ATC), composed of the U.S. domestic airlines, offers a 5-day ATC Travel Agent Training Program. Attendance is limited to full-time employees of travel agencies which are accredited to sell domestic airline tickets. This course is given in a hotel at the Los Angeles International Airport. The employee, or his agency, pays a fee covering instruction, hotel room, and meals, but transportation to and from Los Angeles is provided free by the sponsoring airlines.

The subjects taught in this ATC course are:

- *Introduction to the Air Transport Association and Air Traffic Conference*
- *Domestic Official Airline Guide*
- *Official Airline Guide Travel Planner*
- *ATC Travel Agent Handbook*
- *Government Transportation Taxes*
- *Domestic Airline Tariff*
- *Consolidated Air Tour Manual*
- *Standard Ticket Plan and Ticketing*
- *Basic Skills and Techniques of Selling*

In its first seven months of operation, starting late in 1974, the ATC program was completed by more than 800 travel agents, showing how strong a need exists in the industry for this training.

Several colleges also offer curricula which would be beneficial to travel agents and prospective owners of travel agencies. See Appendix B of this book for a listing of those schools.

EMPLOYMENT AND SALARIES

How does one get a job in a travel agency? Jobs in classified advertisement sections of newspapers generally are listed under the heading, "Travel." The majority of the advertisements demand experience in an agency or in similar work for an airline or other carrier or hotel. A newcomer in the field has no chance of filling such positions, but he should look for advertisements for "travel trainee" or for typists, secretaries, bookkeepers, file clerks, switchboard operators, and similar positions.

There are commercial schools in major cities, offering classroom and correspondence courses in the work of the travel agent. Often the course offering is tied in with offers of job placement. The unfortunate fact is that employers seldom believe that people who have taken these courses are qualified to work in their agencies, unless they also have had agency experience.

The trade press of the travel industry also carries advertisements for positions. Among the publications you should check are: *Travel Age East, Travel Age West, Travel Trade, Travel Agent, Travel Weekly,* and *Pacific Travel News.* Most of the advertisements are for experienced personnel, but "trainee" or clerical and typist positions appear occasionally.

Very large travel agencies, such as American Express and Thomas Cook, may be approached directly, because they frequently must hire trainees as other personnel are promoted or moved.

Employment agencies handle jobs in travel, and some are travel-job specialists. One of these is Yours in Travel. Its owner-manager, Jason King, started the agency in 1973. By 1975, his office in New York was still small, but he had branches in Washington and London and affiliate agencies in many North American cities and in the Caribbean. His agency does the hiring for a number of travel wholesalers and multi-branch travel agencies. The salary ranges with which he works range from $125 per week for trainees up to $90,000 per year for travel-agency executives. At mid-1975, Jason King was very optimistic about job prospects in travel agencies and in the travel industry as a whole. He had more travel-agency jobs than qualified applicants, although most of these positions were for experienced personnel.

Average salaries for jobs in travel agencies are: trainee—$125 per week; information clerk—$125-$150; reservations clerk—$125-$160; typist, file clerk, and switchboard operator—$125-$150; fully qualified travel agent with two years' experience—$175 and up, depending on the size, location, and business of the agency. Managers of branch agencies receive $200-$300 per week, as do department heads in large agencies, although these figures could be much higher in large companies. The department head for a large travel wholesaler could earn $20,000 per year.

Just as in any other job, there are certain disadvantages associated with working for a travel agency or being a travel agent. The business is seasonal, making it necessary for some employees to be laid off for a part of every year. Pleasure travel is considered a luxury by most people; therefore, it is often one of the first things to be cut from the family budget when there is an economic downturn. Agents can cope with a minor economic downturn by scheduling clients for relatively inexpensive forms of travel, but in a very serious recession, travel agencies may be forced out of business.

For employees just starting in the travel agency business, there is a great deal of detail work, which some people do not enjoy. Travel agents also deal with the public constantly, and a few travelers, haughty, supercilious, and demanding, are very hard to please. At peak seasons, a travel agent often must work very long hours, and he is constantly being interrupted by clients telephoning or appearing at his office.

Despite the best efforts of travel agents, travel arrangements can be upset by such unexpected distant events as a strike of airline stewardesses in Iceland or of airline mechanics in Paris, or an earthquake in Nicaragua or Greece. The agent then must work frantically to save what he can of an itinerary and re-plan the rest.

Because of the allure of travel, many young people are attracted to jobs in travel agencies. By the law of supply and demand, large supply means low price; therefore, beginning jobs are not well paid. For this reason, personal travel is considered to be part of a travel agency employee's pay.

Examine your reasons for wanting to be a travel agency employee or owner. If the main attraction is personal travel, rethink the matter thoroughly. Could you earn higher pay in another industry and perhaps travel just as much? You would be paying for your travel, of course, but as a paid passenger, you would experience no waiting for hours for space-available seats, nor would you be bumped at the last minute because one more ticket-holding passenger came aboard.

On the other hand, people who stick with an agency can advance to generous salaries, time off when *they* want it, and the pick of their travel desires over most of the world. A travel agent sometimes can please his clients best by pleasing himself. F. C. M. Pauwels, a travel agent who operates the three-person Plaza Travel Service in New York, likes music and the Orient. So as part of his regular work, each year, he leads a tour of music lovers on a three- or four-week tour of European music festivals. He also leads another tour through parts of the Orient that he enjoys most.

SELF-EMPLOYMENT

Should you go into the travel-agency business yourself, as owner, owner-manager, or partner? If you have the capital, it is not difficult, because agencies are always for sale, as owners retire or decide to sell for some other reason. If you are not experienced in the travel-agency field, it would be much better to buy a partnership in a going business rather than buy a business outright and try to operate it from scratch.

What about the possibility of simply renting a store and putting up a sign to say that you're a travel agent? This probably would not work at all, since you would not be accredited to sell the tickets of the major carriers, and, therefore, would have to buy tickets through another agent and split the commissions.

Some travel agents have broken into the business in this way: working on a straight commission basis for a travel agency, they sell transportation and accommodations, splitting the fees with the agency. When they build up enough capital, know-how, and familiarity with the accrediting agencies, they go into business for themselves. Housewives and clubwomen have done the same sort of thing, starting by chartering buses for church and club outings and selling tickets, just as Thomas Cook did at the beginning of his business, and gradually working up to becoming travel wholesalers.

To be an agent of any kind, you have to represent one or more principals. Travel agents represent mainly carriers and purveyors of lodging, food, and other services. Most hotels and tour operators are glad to accept any sale made by a travel agent of their goods and services, but the major carriers have very strict and formal rules about who can sell their tickets. They are grouped into several Conferences, and each Conference has its own rules as to financial stability, experience in the agency business, and personal responsibility.

A travel agency not approved by the Conferences must obtain its tickets through another agency, splitting the commissions. When an established agency is sold, the new owner must qualify for appointment with each of the Conferences.

The domestic airlines' Conference is the Air Traffic Conference of America (ATC), 1709 New York Avenue N.W., Washington, DC 20006. For international airlines, it's the International Air

Transport Association (IATA), IBM Building, 5 Place Ville Marie, Montreal, 113, PQ Canada. Steamship lines are under the Trans-Pacific Passenger Conference (TPPC), 311 California Street, San Francisco, CA 94104, and the International Passenger Ship Association (IPSA), 17 Battery Place, New York, NY 10004. Almost all domestic rail passenger service is now in National Railroad Passenger Corporation (Amtrak), 955 L'Enfant Plaza North S.W., Washington, DC 20024.

Some 75 percent to 80 percent of all air travel, domestic and worldwide, is on tickets sold by travel agents, and the percentage for steamship travel is even higher. Lufthansa German Airlines reports that in the countries that provide it with the highest amount of revenue, 90 percent of tickets are sold by travel agents. This is the reason that so many travel advertisements, especially those of carriers, say, "See your travel agent."

In difficult times, when airlines are counting their pennies, they are apt to rely heavily on travel agencies. A senior vice president of a major U.S. international airline said in 1975, "If a ticket office costs us more than to sell through an agency in that neighborhood, we close the office."

Income for a travel agency consists very largely of commissions. On air tickets, the commission is usually 7 percent to 7½ percent, but on a package tour that includes both air fare and a week or so at a resort, it is usually 10 percent. Ship fare pays the agent 7 percent on a transatlantic passage, 7.5 percent to 10 percent for a long cruise, and 10 percent for a short cruise. Competition among shippers leaving transatlantic travel to enter the short-cruise business in the Caribbean has led to much higher commissions for groups booked out of ports in Florida, the Gulf of Mexico, and the Caribbean. Shore excursions from cruises pay 10 percent, and sightseeing, entertainment, and tourist attractions pay 10 percent for individuals and more for groups. The commission is 10 percent on Amtrak rail fare as well as on long-distance or excursion bus fare. Auto rental pays 10 percent to 20 percent commission. Hotels and motels pay 10 percent to 15 percent for individuals and 20 percent or more for groups. Travel insurance against accidents, loss of baggage, missing a return trip, and so forth pays a commission of up to 33 percent.

Travel agents sometimes charge fees for such noncommissionable services as obtaining visas for a traveler, sending cablegrams and making long-distance telephone calls for last-minute reservations, and for working out especially complicated itineraries. If a carefully planned trip is canceled, an agent is likely to charge a planning fee.

A special type of travel wholesaler is the *tour consolidator,* who arranges the cheapest form of air travel—charter trips. There are usually no hotel or dining arrangements with such trips—only round-trip air transportation. The consolidator charters an airplane, or perhaps a block of seats, and sells transportation through advertisements or, more typically, to clubs or occupational groups which take care of the clerical work and collect the money for the trip. The work of the consolidator requires knowledge of airlines, a willingness to take risks, selling ability, and usually, a fairly large amount of capital. One way to acquire the necessary skills is to work for a consolidator or in the charter department of a scheduled or nonscheduled airline.

For further information about travel agency careers, write to:

American Society of Travel Agents
360 Lexington Avenue
New York, N.Y. 10017

CHAPTER 8

PUBLIC RELATIONS

Persuasion through communication is the job of the public relations professional. More specifically, public relations for travel concerns the relations of corporations, governments, hotels, carriers, resorts, cities, and other organizations with their own employees, business travelers, pleasure travelers, and the public at large. Among the media used by public relations experts to influence people are: newspapers, magazines, books, radio, television, speeches, photographs, advertisements, surveys, exhibitions, charts, receptions, and parties. Workers in public relations may serve inside the organization being publicized, or they may belong to an outside company specializing in public relations for one or many organizations.

From the most ancient times, rulers paid writers and song-smiths to create works that praised the ruler, inspired patriotism, and persuaded people of the worthiness of the current war. One of the functions of organized religion, also, has always been to support the secular ruler.

These were direct, naive public-relations efforts, and there are thousands of similar examples throughout history. But the term *public relations* did not come into use until early in this century. Earlier, the Roman Catholic Church had instituted the word *propaganda* to describe its efforts to mold public opinion in the Counter-Reformation, and *press agents* were employed by both the North and the South in the Civil War to influence European public opinion. *Propaganda* became a dirty word eventually, because people realized that much of it was false. The term *press agent* seldom is used now because of the work of press agents in covering up or glorifying nefarious schemes of the robber barons of U.S. industry in the late 1800s. The ridiculously excessive publicity stunts of press agents for Hollywood stars and other celebrities early in this century also added to their tainted image.

Public relations in its modern context may be said to have started with Ivy L. Lee and Edward L. Bernays. Lee, hired in 1906 as publicity adviser to the Pennsylvania Railroad, began a policy of openness and frankness with reporters. For example, instead of trying to suppress press awareness of a terrible train wreck, he invited reporters to the scene and helped them to determine and report the cause of the accident.

Rather than just accepting orders to write or to suppress news stories, Lee and Bernays both gave advice to their clients. Bernays studied the people he was trying to influence and decided there were several different "publics" to be reached, and each had to be approached in the most effective way. Bernays claimed to be the first to call himself a "counsel on public relations."

In 1927, John W. Hill, a newspaperman, opened a one-man public relations company in Cleveland, Ohio. His firm, Hill and Knowlton, has become the largest public relations firm in the world, with offices in New York and seven other U.S. cities, as well as in ten European and Asian cities. Mr. Hill, now chairman of the board of Hill and Knowlton, says:

> "Since the aim of public relations is to inform and convince, the good public relations person has a talent both for understanding and for telling. He enjoys explaining things to others and, like a good debater, wants to persuade. The public relations person thus tends to have an aptitude for expression. He is likely to be a good writer or speaker. Choosing the right word at the right time is of real importance to him, for he is sensitive to people's responses. The

Public relations activities range from writing and graphic design to tour management.

good public relations person has curiosity and thoroughness, too. To convince others, he must himself know; and to know, he has to dig. Thus the good public relations person has factual knowledge, but knows people, too—how and why they react, when and how to present his message. He must be concerned equally with the big problem and the small detail."

OPPORTUNITIES FOR WOMEN AND MINORITIES

Rea W. Smith, formerly a partner in a public relations firm in Memphis, is now administrative vice president of the Public Relations Society of America, Inc. in New York, where she heads a large staff. She writes in *Business World:*

"Historically, there has been less discrimination against women in public relations than in many other business fields. Women have been rising to the top rungs in public relations ever since the mid-40s. The current head of public relations for Rockefeller Center in New York is a woman, and her predecessor, who retired after 20 years in the position, was also a woman. In addition, there are hundreds of women who own their own counseling firms."

And opportunities for minorities? Rea Smith continues:

"The field has a crying need for Black talent, not just for those people who can develop improved relationships with the Black community, but also for those who can fulfill community relations and product publicity with all segments of the public, young and old."

The Society of American Travel Writers has 300 Active members (writers, photographers, and broadcasters; on staffs of publications or free-lance); it also has 300 Associate members, who are all in public relations. Of these, 60 are women, many of whom head their own public relations firms and work for one or several travel accounts. Some head public-relations divisions for states, for major hotel chains, for individual hotels and resorts, or for airlines. Several represent national tourist offices of foreign governments in the United States. Women's worth is recognized in public relations, and women are building themselves a larger and larger place in the field.

As the Public Relations Society points out,

"Public relations, at its best, does not only tell an organization's 'story' to its publics. The public relations practitioner also helps shape his organization and the way it performs. Through research, feedback communications and evaluation, the practitioner should find out the concerns and expectations of the organization's various publics and explain them to its management. A responsible—and effective—public relations program should be based on the understanding and support of its publics."

JOB DUTIES

There can be a great deal of variety in public relations work. The functions of the public relations agency or division can be broken down into eight specific kinds of work:

- *Research and evaluation*
- *Defining goals and planning public relations campaigns*
- *Building working relationships*
- *Writing and editing*
- *Dissemination of information*
- *Production of communications*
- *Special events*
- *Public speaking*

Research and evaluation involves gathering together all the available facts that will be necessary to a firmly based public relations effort, then narrowing down the focus to concentrate on areas where changes are desired and can be effected. Library research, personal conversations, interviews with key persons, and broad surveys of public opinion are some of the methods used in this process. At the conclusion of a public relations campaign, the results are studied and evaluated, and lessons may be learned for future efforts.

Defining goals of a public relations campaign avoids waste of effort and money. At this point, plans are made for the amount of money to be spent on each main part of the project and for particular persons to be employed to get the message across in certain quarters. For example, a campaign to bring more tourists to Hawaii might entail sending a troupe of hula dancers and singers to perform at businessmen's luncheon meetings in the 25 largest U.S. cities, or sending some Hawaiian swimming champions to perform at swimming meets around the country. The cooperation of persons outside the public-relations office must be obtained well in advance, and they must understand their job as ambassadors with a message.

Building working relationships is essential in public relations. Much of the effectiveness of campaigns depends upon favors given and received, information provided on the basis of personal friendship, and newspaper space or broadcast time made available because an editor or broadcaster likes and trusts a public relations person. Inside his own company, a public relations worker sometimes must work through the personnel department, the legal department, or the marketing department, and his effectiveness is in direct ratio to his personal acceptability.

Writing and editing form a major part of public relations work because print is the communications medium most often used. Among the writings of public relations people are press releases, brochures, pamphlets, booklets, annual reports, articles for trade magazines, statistics, survey results, technical data, newsletters, shareholder reports, employee publications—also film scripts, and speeches to be given by key personnel. Writing that is clear, lively, and effective in putting a message across will be an important part of any public relations work. As a matter of fact, many a person who writes well and wants to be a novelist sooner or later finds himself in public relations, where he is likely to be better paid (and more regularly) than he would be for writing novels.

Dissemination of information to the appropriate editors of the relevant print and broadcast media is an essential chain in communicating the messages of public relations to its publics. Keeping open the channels to these editors requires a knowledge of their needs, their schedules, and their toleration and cooperation. People in public relations do their best to be known, liked, and trusted by editors.

Production includes all the techniques of art, photography, layout, typography, printing, cinema, and other means of putting the message across. Public relations workers must work with specialists in these fields and must know enough about the techniques to see that they are used with utmost effectiveness.

Special events may take thousands of forms—a state tourist promotion director may invite a dozen writers on a tour of his state in hopes of getting them to write and sell favorable articles. A state such as Virginia may host a party for several hundred writers and editors in New York and show a promotional film to increase their interest in Virginia. An essay contest on local history may be held for high school students in order to obtain newspaper publicity for local historical shrines when the winners are awarded their prizes. News conferences, travel shows, ski shows, boat shows, camping shows, wildwater canoe races, and many kinds of demonstrations of equipment also are used to promote travel. Public relations people may do the original planning for these events, then obtain the cooperation of the principals who speak, compete, or otherwise earn the interest of the public. Finally, the public relations people prepare news stories and reports about the event, easing the way of reporters writing their own stories.

Public speaking is often important in public relations work. Often, a speech written by a public relations worker is delivered by a politician, company president, or celebrity whose presence makes the event newsworthy. It is an advantage for a public relations worker to be an adept public speaker himself, however. If he is, he often may be asked to represent a principal of his company or government who cannot attend all the meetings at which he is invited to speak.

Public relations work is often frantic. If ghetto riots in a city cause prospective visitors to cancel reservations in the whole region, public relations workers must spread the word that areas outside the ghetto are not affected. An earthquake, a hurricane, a political coup, or an outbreak of disease can cause similar reactions and must be countered by public relations. So there is night work, travel during personal time to the site of the difficulty, statements from authorities to be quoted to the press, etc. An air crash always gets headlines and inevitably causes a drop-off in bookings on the airline. Public relations people for the carrier have to work around the clock for weeks after a crash, trying to restore the reputation of the carrier in the minds of the traveling public.

Ideally, a public relations program is based on solid research, evaluation of facts, and determination of goals and schedules. Its various steps are planned for a period of a year to several years in advance.

Consider, for example, an island in the Caribbean or Mediterranean, for which a U.S. public relations agency is engaged to promote tourism. The island has only one hotel, small and very luxurious, but it has an ambitious construction program. In the first year, the agency might arrange visits by a number of celebrities to the one hotel, to build it up in the public mind as a "jet-set hideaway." As the island constructed the necessary infrastructure for development, such as water, sewage, and utility systems, the agency would report these items in the professional travel press, so travel agents would be reminded continually of a new mass market to come. As new hotels were completed, the agency and the hotels would cooperate in holding highly publicized opening parties and celebrations, and shortly thereafter would bring in hundreds of travel agents on free or low-cost familiarization tours. Then package deals with airlines, hotels, and other services would be developed and publicized. Meanwhile, articles about the island's food would be sent to food editors, articles on crafts, history, sports, architecture, native habits, shows, and anything else of news interest would go to appropriate editors. The volume of news releases that can keep flooding out continually about even a little island is staggering.

This volume of press releases causes another problem. Everyday, travel editors on metropolitan newspapers receive one or two mail bags of publicity material. They cannot possibly print more than one percent of it, so the public relations writer has to use all his ingenuity to make his releases and pictures out-of-the-ordinary and distinctive enough to make an editor want to use them.

EDUCATION AND EMPLOYMENT

The young person aiming toward a professional career in public relations should consider graduation from college essential. Many of today's top people in the field arrived by way of journalism, and they consider a degree in journalism, plus a year or two of experience on a newspaper, the best preparation for the field. However, specific education for public relations has been expanding rapidly. In 1974, more than 300 colleges and universities offered at least one course in public relations, and over 80 colleges and 30 graduate schools had degree programs or special curricula in which public relations was an important part of a degree program. Collegiate public relations curricula may be found in schools of journalism, communications, education, and business administration. Programs leading to a master's degree in public relations are given in colleges in Georgia, Indiana, Massachusetts, New Jersey, and New York. Colleges in California, Georgia, Massachusetts, New York, and Ohio offer bachelor degree programs.

The outlook for public relations workers is favorable, because the industry keeps growing as businesses add public relations departments and independent agencies expand their activities. There are over 85,000 public relations workers, of whom almost one-third are women. Outside of four major U.S. cities, they are rather thinly spread, because more than half of them work in New York, Los Angeles, Chicago, and Washington.

Salaries in public relations work cover a very broad range, from a lower-than-average beginner's level of $6,000, up to $75,000 or more for a corporate vice president in charge of public relations. U.S. Department of Labor statistics show that in 1972, starting salaries for college-trained men in public relations averaged $9,000, and for women $6,900. As anti-discrimination laws take effect, this kind of disparity in beginners' salaries is diminishing.

Directors of public relations in medium-sized firms earn from $15,000 to $30,000, and in large companies from $20,000 to $50,000. Their median income was $21,000 in 1972, and top practitioners in corporations were earning $25,000 to over $75,000. An account representative in a public relations firm can earn over $20,000, assuming prime responsibility for relations between his company and a client. People in government public relations and in nonprofit organizations are likely to earn less than the figures cited above, but they also are likely to have more time off on paid vacations as well as a somewhat less hectic life.

Brochures on careers in public relations and a list of colleges offering public relations programs are available from:

> Public Relations Society of America, Inc.
> PRSA Career Guidance
> 845 Third Avenue
> New York, NY 10022

CHAPTER 9

RECREATION

With the increase of leisure time in America and Europe, the proliferation of resorts and sports areas, and the growth of the National Park System, demand for recreation leaders and administrators has grown tremendously during the last few decades. It is likely that this growth will continue in the future. The number of recreation workers in 1972 was about 55,000 (in year-round jobs), nearly half of whom were women. By 1980, the number of jobs in the field is expected to reach 1.4 million.

Public and private support of recreation, although expanding rapidly now, is far from new. The stadium in ancient Greece, the amphitheater in Rome, public gardens, parks, zoos, swimming pools, baths, playgrounds, gymnasiums, opera houses, theaters, dance halls, athletic fields—all attest to man's inveterate devotion to recreation.

Since World War II, the number of hours in the average worker's week have been reduced, vacations have become longer, more holidays have been observed, and the moving of holidays to Mondays or Fridays has increased holiday travel. As of 1974, Congress had enlarged the National Park System to over 30 million acres in 308 parks, with such notable additions as National Seashores on all three coasts. Many states also have devoted much more land to parks, and commercial campgrounds have sprung up around a majority of national and state parks to accommodate constantly overflowing crowds of campers. As a consequence of this growth, whole new industries have been established to manufacture recreation vehicles, houseboats, camping gear, snow skis and water skis, hang gliders, and dozens of other kinds of recreation equipment. New recreational villages have sprung up—second-home communities adjacent to ski areas, beaches, golf courses, tennis compounds, and primitive forests. All of this explains why the need for recreation workers is expanding so rapidly.

JOB DUTIES

What specific jobs do recreation workers perform? They teach dancing and lead social get-togethers to help people meet each other at resorts. They lead calisthenic sessions on beaches and in gymnasiums, aiding people in keeping fit or losing weight. They serve as lifeguards, swimming, tennis, and golf instructors, and coaches for all sorts of athletic teams. Recreators lead singing groups and impromptu bands and orchestras, and they enlist acting talent and put on plays or musical dramas at resorts.

Some recreation workers concentrate on activities with certain age groups, for instance, teaching skiing to infants aged three years and up, or keeping senior citizens busy with checkers and other sedentary activities. Many recreation workers teach such handcrafts as leatherwork, beadwork, basket weaving, macrame, batik, sewing, crocheting, weaving, model building, and dozens of others.

Recreation workers can be divided into three major groups, according to their responsibilities. In the first group, consisting of camp counselors and recreation leaders, the work consists of *teaching people to do things* they can enjoy in their leisure time and *leading* them in sports and games.

The second group consists of *specialists* in particular activities. In a large camp for young people, one specialist might spend all of his or her time teaching people how to make things of leather, holding several classes each day. Another such specialist is the golf professional at a resort or country club. Recreation workers who have enough experience and enough capital sometimes start their own businesses such as camps, hobby shops, outfitters, trail-guide services, boat-rental services, whitewater rafting services, and craft instruction schools.

Above these two groups are members of the third group, the *supervisors and administrators* of recreation programs, summer camps, shipboard passenger activity programs, and the directors of city parks and recreation departments and of leisure programs for nonprofit organizations, corporations, institutions, and the armed services.

EDUCATION AND EMPLOYMENT

Employment conditions for recreation workers are usually very pleasant; they are helping people to enjoy life and to learn simple skills which give a feeling of accomplishment. Generally, a recreation worker should be an outgoing, gregarious person who is interested in other people and eager to help and to teach. The work should bring pleasure to the recreator, because he must work when most other people are at leisure—evenings, weekends, and the summer vacation months. Having time off when most people are working, the recreation worker may have difficulty finding recreation for himself outside his work with others.

Summer recreation programs give employment to more than twice as many people as are regularly employed full-time in recreation work. Summer jobs as camp counselors and recreation leaders give an excellent start to the person intending to make a career in recreation, providing the indispensable experience necessary to obtain a full-time job in the field.

High school graduation and some camping experience is generally sufficient to obtain a summer job as camp counselor.

Other part-time recreation jobs are filled by college students with training in physical education or aptitude for such specialties as music, drama, art, gymnastics, crafts, botany, ecology, boating, sailing, hiking, mineralogy, horseback riding, and swimming.

To obtain a year-round position in recreation, considerable experience is highly desirable, as is graduation from at least a two-year college and, preferably, a four-year one. The profession of directing recreation is a young one which is growing rapidly, and as it grows, educational requirements will become more stringent. The young person with foresight will complete four years of college and go on to obtain a master's degree and perhaps even a doctorate, in order to avoid being prevented from advancing later because of a lack of formal educational credentials. Many recreation workers specializing in music, drama, dance, and art have graduate degrees.

The first two years of college should provide a broad general background, covering sciences, sociology, communication, languages, history, and perhaps philosophy. The last two years are taken up with more specialized courses in leadership, group dynamics, recreation programming, sports of many kinds, safety and health protection in recreation, art, crafts, dance, and field recreation leadership under supervision.

Graduate work might well include courses such as business administration, since program directors must prepare budgets, allocate funds, and conduct their recreation programs in a businesslike fashion. Other graduate courses should concentrate mainly on the recreator's specific area of interest.

Salaries for recreation workers vary broadly. Some camp counselors in summer jobs may receive little more than room and board, while workers in other camps may receive attractive salaries. Salaries for permanent positions start at about $6,000 to $8,000 per year for a person with a bachelor's degree, and up to $10,000 for those with bachelor's degrees plus experience. A master's degree increases the starting salary by $1,000 to $2,000 per year. Supervisors earn up to about $13,000, and recreation directors' salaries can go as high as $25,000.

Hours of work average 40 per week, but can rise far beyond that because of the irregularity of recreation workers' schedules. Recreation employers generally give their workers two to four weeks' annual vacation, as well as sick leave, hospital insurance, and other fringe benefits. As the recreation field enlarges, it becomes more stabilized and secure for workers.

To find a summer camp job, or for information on a career in camping, write:

> American Camping Association
> Bradford Woods
> Martinsville, Indiana 46151

For more information on careers in recreation, colleges with recreation curricula, and employment opportunities, write:

> National Recreation and Parks Association
> 1601 North Kent Street
> Arlington, Virginia 22209

See Appendix B for a listing of schools offering curricula in recreation leadership.

CHAPTER 10

TRAVEL WRITING

A "traveler's tale," in English slang a few generations ago, meant a tall story—a highly colored and exaggerated account of adventures in exotic and faraway lands. Most of the world's literatures have included such reports. Homer's *Odyssey,* dating from about 850 B.C., not only relates the adventures of Odysseus (Ulysses) over the 20 years it took him to come home from the Trojan War, but also describes accurately many parts of the Mediterranean world that he visited.

One of the world's most fascinating travel classics is *The Book of Marco Polo.* Fortunately for the world, this Venetian man of action, after his epochal journeys across Asia and his 24 years in the service of Kublai Khan, was taken prisoner in a war between Venice and Genoa. Using his carefully written travel notebooks, in 1298 he dictated to a fellow captive, the scribe Rustigielo of Pisa, the book that disclosed Cathay to Europe. Christopher Columbus had a copy of this book and made notations on more than 70 pages. His object, when he sailed in 1492, was to reach Marco Polo's Cathay.

Another monumental travel writer was Richard Hakluyt of England, who became archdeacon of Westminster and is buried in Westminster Abbey. Between 1582 and 1600 he wrote several books, chief of which is his *Principall Navigations, Voiages, and Discoveries of the English Nation,* describing all the great seaborne expeditions of English captains to America, the Arctic, the Pacific, and around the world.

If only some chronicler had joined the fishing expeditions of early Portuguese, French, English, and Scandinavian fishermen, we might know much more about ancient landings in North America. It is suspected that there was fishing on the Grand Banks off Newfoundland and Nova Scotia as much as a thousand years ago.

The first important analysis of America and its life is *De la democratie en Amerique,* published in 1835, by Comte Alexis de Tocqueville. Sent to examine the U.S. penitentiary system for the French government, de Tocqueville wrote his report on prisons, then in *Democracy in America,* he described American life with such penetration as had never been applied before, and seldom since. He perceived that the great difference between Europe and America was the American insistence upon equality, and he shows how this affected every facet of life in America, from emergent literature to science, religion, philosophy, the arts, language, business, the family, the military, and manners. He didn't care much for our ancestors' manners, but he foresaw that the influence of democracy would bring about the emancipation of women.

De Tocqueville's work would not be considered travel writing by some persons—those who believe that travel writing concerns itself solely with the traveler's transportation, accommodations, shopping, and recreation. But, in reality, this is the very best kind of travel writing, because de Tocqueville delivers that most precious gift—insight.

The insight of the travel writer can bring the reader to feel kinship with people of another land and another race, by showing the universal emotions and motivations behind customs that are strange, even bizarre. An alert travel writer is always attuned to the subtle emanations of a new place and its people. Every bit of feeling that a place arouses in a travel writer must be savored, perhaps analyzed, but certainly fully realized, so that the writer can express it in such a way as to make the reader feel it as well.

Two men who strongly influenced the development of guidebooks as we know them today were John Murray of London and Karl Baedeker of Koblenz, Germany. John Murray (1808-1892) was the third of a distinguished line of publishers, all bearing the same name. He wrote a series of *Handbooks* on the Netherlands, Belgium, France, the Rhine, South Germany, and Switzerland.

Karl Baedeker (1801-1859) started a printing plant in Koblenz in 1827. Under an arrangement with John Murray, he published a pocket-sized guidebook on the Rhine, Belgium, and the Netherlands in 1839. He subsequently brought out guides covering most of Europe and parts of North America and the Orient. These books were so reliable and thorough that the name Baedeker became a synonym for the word guidebook. The era of exaggerated "travelers' tales" had ended. Baedeker started the practice of marking with one or more stars in his books places of special interest or attraction, so travelers with little time could determine quickly what to see. "Starred in Baedeker" soon came to mean "well worth visiting." These *Baedekers* were published from the first in German, French, and English, and this helped them to gain extremely wide readership.

In our own time, the mantle of Baedeker graces the shoulders of Eugene Fodor, a native Hungarian who is now a U.S. citizen. He was editing travel books by 1936 and begun publishing *Fodor's Guides* in Paris after World War II. He moved his headquarters to Litchfield, Connecticut, in the 1960s. For each of his books, Fodor generally uses a team of several authors and researchers. Whenever possible, Fodor employs experts residing in the country described by the book.

Quite different are the highly personal guidebooks exemplified by Myra Waldo's *Travel and Motoring Guide to Europe* and *Fielding's Travel Guide to Europe,* by Temple Fielding. These popular guidebooks, which are revised annually, depend for their attraction on the readers' confidence that they can rely upon the taste and preferences of Myra Waldo and Temple Fielding.

Arthur Frommer, after traveling through Europe as inexpensively as possible with his wife, wrote *Europe on $5 a Day,* an inexpensive paperback book. The title's assertion that travel could be very inexpensive doubtless inspired many Americans to visit Europe. For millions of young people, it was a bible of essential information, carried around Europe until it was dogeared and tattered. It was such a success that Frommer started a publishing house, and he keeps a number of authors busy writing and updating over 40 titles. Each book is written by a single writer or a team of two writers.

Many readers seek excitement, exotic scenes, and escapist literature which takes them out of their daily routines. Travel books do this, with descriptions of true adventure in jungle exploration or mountain climbing, treasure hunting or visiting natives of lost civilizations, archeological exploration or sailing trips across an ocean on a raft. This kind of escapist nonfiction permits armchair travel and is at the opposite end of the spectrum of travel writing from the step-by-step Baedeker.

In between these opposites are many kinds of books on outdoor life, hunting and fishing, camping, ecology, folklore, local crafts, transportation, skiing, boating, history, cruising, flying, gliding, and so forth. Some of these are written to amaze or amuse the reader, and others to give the reader practical advice and instruction. Most publishers put out at least occasional travel books, and some specialize in travel subjects.

As travel has become more widespread, the amount of travel coverage in magazines and newspapers has increased. Travel is a major interest, and people do more traveling every year. Another reason for the increase in the number of travel articles is that travel advertising has been increasing from year to year. A magazine or newspaper carrying a great deal of travel advertising must carry a commensurate amount of travel writing; otherwise, readers do not look at the advertising. If a Sunday newspaper's travel section had only advertisements, most people would discard it unread.

OPPORTUNITIES FOR WOMEN

Opportunities for women in travel writing are every bit as good as those for men. A check of the roster of the Society of American Travel Writers (SATW) for 1975 shows that one-third of its Active members were women. Active members include free-lance writers, photographers, broadcasters, staff travel writers, photographers on newspapers and magazines, and travel editors in magazines, newspapers, and book-publishing houses. It might be noted that SATW's national president and the presidents of three of its six regional chapters in 1975 were women.

EMPLOYMENT AND SALARIES

While travel writing is important to readers, and therefore essential to magazines and newspapers, it is not a lucrative field. The reason is an ancient economic one, the law of supply and demand. There are so many people willing to write articles on travel for little or nothing, and public relations people supply so much in the way of free articles and pictures, that a newspaper editor on a slim budget may decide to buy no articles at all, relying solely on free material.

During the economic slowdown of the mid-70s, when newspapers, besides suffering from general inflation, suffered a shortage of newsprint (paper) and greatly increased costs of newsprint, ink, and labor, many newspapers that had been regular buyers of travel articles from free-lancers completely stopped buying. They had their travel editors write articles, they used free articles from public relations sources, and they used articles provided by the wire services at very low cost.

This makes travel writing on a full-time free-lance basis a highly insecure profession. As a result, there are very few full-time free-lance travel writers. Many a man or woman who would like to be a full-time free-lance travel writer finds it necessary to do some writing in public relations or in other fields in order to survive.

Staff positions as *travel editor* or assistant travel editor on a magazine or newspaper are much more secure. Almost never, however, is a person given such a position because he or she has trained for it or is a specialist in travel. On newspapers, unfortunately, the travel editorship sometimes is given to an aging reporter who is coasting toward retirement, as a reward for past service. He gets an opportunity to do some traveling and to write about it, but he does not regard such writing very seriously, and, consequently, his readers are shortchanged.

To help combat such attitudes, the Society of American Travel Writers was founded in 1956. Its two primary goals are: to convince publishers that responsible travel reporting is an essential editorial service, an inescapable obligation to readers in this age of rising leisure and discretionary income; and to build joint strength of travel writers in support of their elemental function in the travel industry—as true spokesmen and travel critics for the average traveler.

The first president of the Society of American Travel Writers was Peter Celliers, who for several years held a piquant pair of jobs, as travel editor of both *Playboy* and *Modern Bride* at the same time. Now senior partner of a public relations agency, Celliers notes with distress that more than half of the U.S. newspapers and magazines that purport to cover travel still do so without any professional consistency.

Travel writing, for most free-lance travel writers, does not earn enough to cover the costs of the necessary travel. Recognizing this, and hoping to obtain coverage of their attractions or facilities, airlines, resorts, hotels, railroads, and state or national governments often invite travel writers on a press trip and cover part or all of their expenses. Although some critics feel that press trips constitute "bribery" of writers, it must be remembered that newspapers pay expenses of any reporters who must travel to cover any kind of story. Additionally, if such trips were eliminated for the professional free-lancer, the travel writing business would be left to business travelers, pleasure travelers who have some flair for writing, and others to whom travel writing is a sideline.

Writing about press trips, Richard Dunlop, author of numerous travel books and a former president of the Society of American Travel Writers, says:

> "I cannot imagine that any responsible public relations person who works for an honorable client, whether it be a hotel company, airline, state, or foreign government, thinks he can buy a respected travel writer by inviting him on a press trip. Nor would a travel writer of stature go on such a trip if he thought he was being bought.
>
> "I have always felt free to write exactly what I thought of the areas I visited on press trips, and I believe that all travel writers who are members of the SATW should take the same attitude."

Another difficulty for the young person trying to become a full-time professional free-lance travel writer is that the star system is in effect at most of the best magazines. An editor wants to publish as many articles by celebrities as he can get, so their names can be printed on the cover to help sell the magazine. This makes it difficult for a newcomer to break into the field and to sell enough articles to keep going.

This look at some of the problems shows that free-lance travel writing is, in general, an insecure field. For those with abundant talent and persistence, however, it is a fascinating way to earn a living.

TRAVEL EDITORS

A position as *travel editor* of a magazine or newspaper is much more secure than that of a free-lancer, because there is a regular salary, regular hours in the publication's offices, and in the case of most metropolitan newspapers, a union contract to regulate working conditions. The Newspaper Guild, which is the union for reporters and editors, has been quite militant about obtaining good salaries and other benefits for its members.

Travel writing and travel editing generally are not recognized as specialties open to beginning reporters and editors in the newspaper world, so the neophyte must begin as a general reporter or copy editor. As more educational institutions develop curricula in TTT (transportation, travel, and tourism), newspapers may begin to place TTT graduates in assignments that cover these subjects. Since the colleges with TTT generally do not require courses in writing, newspapers may obtain TTT specialists from among journalism graduates who have minored in TTT.

There are so few magazine travel editors that it is difficult to generalize about them, but it can be said that a college education is required for such work. Some travel editors are journalism graduates, but many are graduates in fine arts. For both newspapers and magazines, the master's degree is becoming more important.

The work of a travel editor varies greatly from one publication to another. On some newspapers and magazines, the travel editor is actually the sole travel writer and writes all the travel coverage. Richard Joseph, for example, has been travel editor of *Esquire* since 1946. He generally writes two articles for each issue, and *Esquire* seldom buys any other travel articles. Joseph does a great deal of traveling to gather material.

On a metropolitan newspaper that buys 10 to 30 travel articles each week, the travel editor's job is completely different. He generally works regular shift hours and is inundated with unsolicited articles, queries about prospective articles, and press releases from carriers, hotels, and attractions. Selecting articles, corresponding with travel writers, editing articles, and coping with problems of layout, photography, and deadlines are activities requiring just about all his time, so he has little opportunity to travel himself. On the prosperous newspapers, there are one to four assistant travel editors, so the work can get done even if two of them are traveling on assignment. On the papers with lower budgets, the travel editor may have no funds for personal travel or for buying articles. He relies upon public relations press releases and may write an occasional article on places he visits during his vacations.

To become any kind of a travel writer, editor, or broadcaster today, a college education is essential, and graduate degrees help. A travel photographer does not need college training, but must have a great deal of technical expertise, as well as flair for the work. The competition in this work is very stiff—a magazine editor selecting photographs to illustrate an article often will have 100 to 200 or more offered, of which one to five may be used.

Further information about opportunities on newspapers and salaries for graduates of journalism schools, also a list of scholarships, fellowships, assistantships, and loans for journalism students may be obtained from:

The Newspaper Fund, Inc.
Box 300
Princeton, New Jersey 08540

Current union wage scale information can be requested from:

The Newspaper Guild
Research Department
1125 15th Street N.W.
Washington, DC 20005

Opportunities for women in newspapers, magazines, and broadcasting are described in information from:

Women in Communications, Inc.
8305 A Shoal Creek Boulevard
Austin, Texas 78758

APPENDIX A

RECOMMENDED READING

Arco Editorial Board. *Bus Operator: Conductor.* New York: Arco, 1970.

Barish, Mort, and Michaela M. Mole. *Mort's Guide to 100,000 Vacation Jobs.* Princeton, N.J.: C.M.G. Publishing Company, 1975'.

Brownell, George G. *Travel Agency Management.* Birmingham: Southern University Press, 1975.

Dukas, Peter. *Front Office Management and Operation.* Dubuque, Iowa: William C. Brown, 1970.

Evert, Judy. *Introduction to Hospitality-Recreation Careers.* Bloomington, Illinois: McKnight Publishing Company, 1975.

Ford, Norman D. *How to Travel and Get Paid For It.* Greenlawn, N.Y.: Harian Press, 1970.

Gold, Faye, and Raymond J. Grandfield. *Working in the Transportation Industry.* New York: Fairchild Publications, 1974.

Henkin, Shepard. *Opportunities in Public Relations.* New York: Vocational Guidance Manuals, 1964.

____ . *Opportunities In The Hotel and Motel Business.* New York: Vocational Guidance Manuals, 1967.

Kalt, Nathan. *Introduction to the Hospitality Industry.* Indianapolis: Howard W. Sams Company, 1971.

Lundberg, Donald E. *The Hotel and Restaurant Business.* Boston: Cahners Books, 1974.

Morton, Alexander C. *Airline Guide to Stewardess and Steward Careers.* New York: Arco, 1975.

Scribner, Kimball J. *Your Future as a Pilot.* New York: Arco, 1968.

Smith, Johni. *How to Be a Flight Stewardess.* Hollywood, Calif.: Pan American Navigation Service, 1974.

Taylor, W. L. *Pilot's Guide to an Airline Career.* Glendale, Calif.: Aviation Book Company, 1975.

U.S. Bureau of Labor Statistics. *Occupational Outlook Handbook.* Washington: Government Printing Office (latest edition).

Vallen, Jerome J. *Check In–Check Out! Principles of Effective Front Office Management.* Dubuque, Iowa: William C. Brown, 1974.

APPENDIX B

COLLEGES OFFERING DEGREES OR COURSES IN THE FIELD OF TRAVEL

ADVERTISING

Alabama
University of Alabama
Dept. of Journalism
University 35486

Arizona
Arizona State University
College of Business Admin.
Tempe 85281

Northern Arizona Univ.
Dept. of Journalism
Flagstaff 86001

Arkansas
Univ. of Arkansas at
Little Rock
Dept. of Advertising
Little Rock 72204

California
California State Univ.
Dept. of Journalism
Fresno 93710

California State Univ.
Dept. of Communications
Fullerton 92634

California State Univ.
Dept. of Journalism and
Advertising
San Jose 95192

San Francisco State Univ.
Dept. of Marketing
San Francisco 94132

Colorado
Univ. of Colorado
School of Journalism
Boulder 80302

Connecticut
Univ. of Bridgeport
Dept. of Journalism/
Communications
Bridgeport 06602

Florida
Florida State Univ.
Dept. of Advertising and
Public Relations
Tallahassee 32306

Florida Technological Univ.
Dept. of Communication
Orlando 32816

Univ. of Florida
College of Journalism and
  Communication
Gainesville 32611

Univ. of South Florida
Dept. of Mass Communications
Tampa 33620

Georgia
Univ. of Georgia
School of Journalism
Athens 30601

Illinois
Northern Illinois Univ.
Dept. of Journalism
DeKalb 60115

Northwestern Univ.
Dept. of Advertising
Evanston, 60201

Roosevelt Univ.
Dept. of Marketing
Chicago 60604

Southern Illinois Univ.
School of Journalism
Carbondale 62901

Univ. of Illinois
Dept. of Advertising
Urbana 61801

Indiana
Ball State Univ.
Center for Journalism
Muncie 47306

Indiana University
Dept. of Journalism
Bloomington 47401

Iowa
Drake University
School of Journalism
Des Moines 50311

Univ. of Iowa
Dept. of Business Admin.
Iowa City 52242

Kansas
Univ. of Kansas
School of Journalism
Lawrence 66045

Kentucky
Univ. of Kentucky
School of Communication
Lexington 40506

Western Kentucky Univ.
Dept. of Mass Communications
Bowling Green 42101

Louisiana
Louisiana State Univ.
School of Journalism
Baton Rouge 70803

Maryland
Univ. of Maryland
College of Journalism
College Park 20742

Massachusetts
Boston University
School of Public Communica-
  tion
Boston 02215

Michigan
Ferris State College
Dept. of Marketing and
  Retailing
Big Rapids 49307

Michigan State Univ.
Dept. of Advertising
East Lansing 48823

Western Michigan Univ.
Dept. of Marketing
Kalamazoo 49001

Minnesota
Univ. of Minnesota
School of Journalism and
　Mass Communication
Minneapolis 55455

Mississippi
Univ. of Southern Mississippi
Depts. of Marketing and
　Communications
Hattiesburg 39401

Missouri
Lincoln University
Dept. of Journalism
Jefferson City 65101

Univ. of Missouri
School of Journalism
Columbia 65201

Montana
Univ. of Montana
School of Journalism
Missoula 59801

Nebraska
Creighton University
Depts. of Marketing and
　Journalism
Omaha 68178

Univ. of Nebraska
School of Journalism
Lincoln 68508

Univ. of Nebraska at
　Omaha
Dept. of Journalism
Omaha 68101

Nevada
Univ. of Nevada
Dept. of Journalism
Reno 89507

New Jersey
Fairleigh Dickinson Univ.
Dept. of Marketing
Rutherford 07070

Fairleigh Dickinson Univ.
Dept. of Marketing
Teaneck 07666

Fairleigh Dickinson Univ.
Dept. of Marketing
Madison 07940

New Mexico
New Mexico State Univ.
Dept. of Journalism and
　Mass Communications
Las Cruces 88003

New York
City Univ. of New York
Dept. of Marketing
The Bernard M. Baruch
　College
155 East 24th Street
New York 10011

Long Island Univ.–
　Brooklyn Center
School of Business Admin.
Brooklyn 11201

Syracuse University
School of Journalism
Syracuse 13210

North Carolina
Univ. of North Carolina
School of Journalism
Chapel Hill 27514

Ohio
Bowling Green State Univ.
Dept. of Marketing
Bowling Green 43403

Univ. of Dayton
Depts. of Marketing and
  Communication Arts
300 College Park Drive
Dayton 45409

Kent State Univ.
School of Journalism
Kent 44242

Ohio University
School of Journalism
Athens 45701

Youngstown State Univ.
Dept. of Advertising and
  Public Relations
Youngstown 44503

Oklahoma
Oklahoma State Univ.
School of Journalism and
  Broadcasting
Stillwater 74074

Univ. of Oklahoma
School of Journalism
Norman 73069

Univ. of Tulsa
Dept. of Communications
Tulsa 74104

Oregon
Univ. of Oregon
School of Journalism
Eugene 97403

Pennsylvania
Pennsylvania State Univ.
School of Journalism
University Park 16802

Rhode Island
Univ. of Rhode Island

Dept. of Marketing Management
Kingston 02881

South Carolina
Univ. of South Carolina
College of Journalism
Columbia 29208

South Dakota
The Univ. of South Dakota
Dept. of Communication
Vermillion 57069

Tennessee
Memphis State Univ.
Depts. of Journalism and
  Marketing
Memphis 38111

Univ. of Tennessee
Dept. of Advertising
Knoxville 37916

Texas
East Texas State Univ.
Dept. of Journalism and
  Graphic Arts
Commerce 75428

Texas Christian Univ.
Dept. of Journalism
Fort Worth 76129

Texas Tech University
Dept. of Mass Communications
Lubbock 79409

Texas Wesleyan College
Dept. of Marketing
Fort Worth 76105

The Univ. of Texas
Dept. of Advertising
Austin 78712

Utah
    Brigham Young Univ.
    Dept. of Communications
    Provo 84601

Virginia
    Virginia Commonwealth Univ.
    Dept. of Mass Communications
    Richmond 23284

Washington
    Univ. of Washington
    School of Communications
    Seattle 98105

West Virginia
    West Virginia Univ.

    School of Journalism
    Morgantown 26506

Wisconsin
    Marquette University
    College of Journalism and
        Dept. of Marketing
    Milwaukee 53233
    Univ. of Wisconsin
    School of Journalism and
        Mass Communication
    Dept. of Marketing
    School of Business
    Madison 53706
    Wisconsin State Univ.
    Dept. of Journalism
    Eau Claire 54701

HOTEL-MOTEL ADMINISTRATION

Arizona
    Arizona State Univ.
    Tempe 85281

California
    City College of San
        Francisco
    Hotel and Restaurant Dept.
    Ocean and Phelan Avenues
    San Francisco 94112

    Mesa College
    7250 Artillery Drive
    San Diego 92111

    Monterey Peninsula College
    School of Food/Lodging/
        Travel Administration
    980 Fremont Avenue
    Monterey 93940

    Orange Coast College
    2701 Fairview Road
    Costa Mesa 92626

Colorado
    Univ. of Denver
    2030 East Evans Street
    Denver 80210

Connecticut
    Manchester Com. College
    Manchester   06040

    Univ. of New Haven
    300 Orange Avenue
    West Haven 06516

Florida
    Broward Junior College
    3501 S.W. Davie Road
    Fort Lauderdale 33314

    Florida International Univ.
    School of Hotel, Food, and
        Travel Services
    Tamiami Trail
    Miami 33144

Florida State Univ.
Tallahassee 32306

Hillsborough Com. College
P.O. Box 22127
Tampa 33622

Miami-Dade Junior College
11380 N.W. 27th Avenue
Miami 33167

Palm Beach Junior College
4200 Congress Street
Lake Worth 33460

St. Petersburg Junior College
St. Petersburg 33710

Valencia Junior College
P.O. Box 3028
Orlando 32809

Hawaii
Univ. of Hawaii at Manoa
School of Travel Industry
Management
1300 Lower Campus Road
Honolulu 96822

Kapiolani Com. College
620 Pensacola Street
Honolulu 96814

Indiana
Indiana Northern Univ.
Box 1000
University Park
Gas City 46933

Purdue University
Lafayette 47907

Univ. of Notre Dame
Hayes-Healy Travel
Management Program
College of Business Admin.
Notre Dame 46556

Iowa
Iowa State Univ.
Ames 50010

Maine
Washington County Voca-
tional-Technical Institute
River Road
Calais 04619

Maryland
Com. College of Baltimore
2901 Liberty Heights Ave.
Baltimore 21215

Montgomery College
51 Mannakee
Rockville 20805

Massachusetts
Univ. of Massachusetts
Amherst 01002

Michigan
Educational Institute of the
American Hotel & Motel
Association (home study
and group study)
Michigan State Univ.
East Lansing 48823

Michigan State Univ.
School of Hotel, Restaurant,
and Institutional Manage-
ment
Eppley Center
East Lansing 48824

Schoolcraft College
18600 Haggerty Road
Livonia 48151

Minnesota
Southwest Minnesota State
College
Marshall 56258

Univ. of Minnesota Technical
College
Crookstone 56716

Missouri
Crowder College
Neosho 64850

Forest Park Com. College
5600 Oakland
St. Louis 63110

Penn Valley Com. College
560 Westport Road
Kansas City 64111

Univ. of Missouri
Columbia 65201

Nebraska
Central Nebraska Vocational-
Technical School
Box 1024
Hastings 68901

Nevada
Univ. of Nevada
College of Hotel Admin.
Las Vegas 89154

New Hampshire
Univ. of New Hampshire
Durham 03820

New Jersey
Atlantic Com. College
Mays Landing 08330

Middlesex County College
Edison 08817

New York
Cornell University
School of Hotel Admin.
Statler Hall
Ithaca 14853

New York City Com. College
300 Jay Street
Brooklyn 11201

Paul Smith's College
Hotel and Resort Management
Dept.
Paul Smiths 12970

State Univ. Agricultural and
Technical College
Delhi 13753

Sullivan County Com. College
South Fallsburg 12779

North Carolina
Appalachian State Univ.
Box 200
Boone 28607

Wilkes Com. College
Drawer 120
Wilkesboro 28697

Oklahoma
Oklahoma State Univ.
School of Hotel and Restaurant
Administration
Stillwater 74074

Oregon
Portland Com. College
12000 S.W. 49th Avenue
Portland 97219

Pennsylvania
Luzerne County Com. College
Wilkes Barre 18702

Pennsylvania State Univ.
University Park 16802

South Carolina
Univ. of South Carolina
Columbia 29208

Texas
Univ. of Houston
Hilton School of Hotel and
Restaurant Management
925 Caroline
Houston 77004

Utah
Utah Technical College
Provo 84601

Virgin Islands
College of the Virgin
Islands
P.O. Box 1826

Charlotte Amalie
St. Thomas 00801

Washington
Washington State Univ.
Hotel Admin. Dept.
Pullman 99163

Wisconsin
Madison Area Tech. College
211 N. Carroll Street
Madison 53703

Univ. of Wisconsin—Stout
Hotel and Restaurant
Management Dept.
Menomonie 54751

PUBLIC RELATIONS

California
San Jose State College
Dept. of Journalism and
Advertising
San Jose 95114

Univ. of Southern California
School of Journalism
Los Angeles 90007

Florida
Florida State Univ.
College of Business
Tallahassee 32306

Georgia
Univ. of Georgia
School of Journalism
Athens 30601

Indiana
Ball State Univ.
Center for Journalism
Muncie 47306

Massachusetts
Boston University
School of Public Communi-
cation
Boston 02215

New Jersey
Glassboro State College
School Information Service
Program
Glassboro 08028

New York
Pace College
Graduate School of
Business Admin.
New York 10038

Syracuse University
School of Journalism
Syracuse 13210

Utica College
Division of Business Admin.
Utica 13502

Ohio
 Ohio University
 College of Communication
 Athens 46701

Youngstown State Univ.
Dept. of Advertising and
 Public Relations
Youngstown 44503

RECREATION LEADERSHIP

Alabama
 Auburn University
 Auburn 36830
 Jefferson State Jr. College
 Birmingham 35215
 Theodore Alfred Lawson
  State Junior College
 Birmingham 35211

Arkansas
 Arkansas Polytechnic College
 Russelville 72802

California
 American River College
 Sacramento 95841
 Antelope Valley College
 Lancaster 93534
 California State College
 Long Beach 90801
 Feather River College
 Quincy 95971
 Foothill College
 Los Altos Hills 94022
 Fresno City College
 Fresno 93704
 Fullerton Junior College
 Fullerton 92034

Glendale College
Glendale 91208

Golden West College
Huntington Beach 92647

Mira Costa College
Oceanside 92054

Monterey Peninsula College
Monterey 93940

Sacramento State College
Sacramento 95819

San Diego City College
San Diego 92101

San Diego Mesa College
San Diego 92111

San Diego State College
San Diego 92115

Southwestern College
Chula Vista 92010

Univ. of California
Davis 95616

Univ. of the Pacific
Stockton 95204

Colorado
 Com. College of Denver—
  West Campus
 Lakewood 80215

 Mesa College
 Grand Junction 81501

University of Northern
 Colorado
Greeley 80631

Connecticut
Northwestern Connecticut
 Com. College
Winsted 06098

Florida
Florida International Univ.
Miami 33144

Florida State Univ.
Tallahassee 32306

Miami-Dade Junior College
Miami 33156

Palm Beach Junior College
Lake Worth 33460

Georgia
DeKalb College
Clarkston 30021

Georgia Southern College
Statesboro 30458

South Georgia College
Douglas 31533

University of Georgia
Athens 30601

Hawaii
Univ. of Hawaii at Manoa
Honolulu 96822

Illinois
College of DuPage
Glen Ellyn 60137

George Williams College
Downers Grove 60515

Moraine Valley Com. College
Palos Hills 60482

Triton College
Rivergrove 60171

Indiana
Indiana Northern Univ.
Gas City 46933

Indiana University
Bloomington 47401

Kentucky
Ashland Com. College
Ashland 41101

Hopkinsville Com. College
Hopkinsville 42240

Louisiana
Northwestern State Univ.
Natchitoches 71457

Maryland
Com. College of Baltimore
Baltimore 21215

Montgomery College at
 Rockville
Rockville 20850

Univ. of Maryland
College Park 20742

Massachusetts
Berkshire Com. College
Pittsfield 01201

Greenfield Com. College
Greenfield 01301

Northeastern University
Boston 02115

Springfield College
Springfield 01109

Michigan
Eastern Michigan Univ.
Ypsilanti 48197

Macomb County Com. College
–Center Campus
Warren 48093

Michigan State Univ.
East Lansing 48823

Wayne State Univ.
Detroit 48202

Minnesota
Mankato State College
Mankato 56001

Normandale Jr. College
Bloomington 55431

North Hennepin State Jr.
College
Minneapolis 55428

Missouri
Central Missouri State College
Warrensburg 64093

Nebraska
Univ. of Nebraska
Omaha 68101

Nevada
Univ. of Nevada
Las Vegas 89154

New York
Columbia University–Teachers
College
New York 10027

Genesee Com. College
Batavia 14020

New York University
New York 10003

State University of New York
–College at Cortland
Cortland 13045

Paul Smith's College
Paul Smiths 12970

Syracuse University
Syracuse 13210

North Carolina
Univ. of North Carolina
Greensboro 27412

Ohio
Kent State Univ.
Kent 44242

Ohio State Univ.
Athens 45701

Oklahoma
Univ. of Tulsa
Tulsa 74104

Pennsylvania
California State College
California 15419

Pennsylvania State Univ.
University Park 16802

Texas
Tarrant County Jr. College
Fort Worth 76119

Texas Woman's Univ.
Denton 76204

Utah
Brigham Young Univ.
Provo 84601

Vermont
Goddard College
Plainfield 05667

Virginia
Radford College
Radford 24141

Virginia Commonwealth Univ.
Richmond 23220

Washington
Bellevue Com. College
Bellevue 98007

Big Bend Com. College
Moses Lake 98837

Everett Com. College
Everett 98201

Highline Com. College
Midway 98031

Univ. of Washington
Seattle 98105

Wisconsin
Univ. of Wisconsin
Madison 53706

RESTAURANT ADMINISTRATION

Alabama
Auburn University
Auburn 36830

Tuskegee Institute
Tuskegee 36083

Arizona
Arizona State Univ.
Tempe 85281

California
Bakersfield College
Bakersfield 93305

City College of San Francisco
Hotel and Restaurant Dept.
Ocean and Phelan Avenues
San Francisco 94112

Contra Costa Jr. College
2600 Mission Bell Drive
San Pablo 94806

Grossmont College
Food Service Management
Department
8800 Grossmont College Dr.
El Cajon 92020

Los Angeles Trade-Technical
College
400 West Washington Blvd.
Los Angeles 90015

Mesa College
7250 Artillery Drive
San Diego 92111

Monterey Peninsula College
School of Food/Lodging/
Travel Admin.
980 Fremont Avenue
Monterey 93940

Moorpark College
7075 Campus Road
Moorpark 93021

Orange Coast College
2701 Fairview Road
Costa Mesa 92626

West Valley College
44 East Latimer Avenue
Campbell 95008

Colorado
Colorado State Univ.
Dept. of Food Science and
Nutrition
Fort Collins 80521

Univ. of Denver
2030 East Evans Street
Denver 80210

Connecticut
Manchester Com. College
Manchester 06040

South Central Com. College
869 Orange Street
New Haven 06511

Univ. of New Haven
300 Orange Avenue
West Haven 06516

Florida

Broward Junior College
3501 S.W. Davie Road
Fort Lauderdale 33314

Florida International Univ.
School of Hotel, Food, and
  Travel Services
Tamiami Trail
Miami 33144

Florida State Univ.
Tallahassee 32306

Hillsborough Com. College
P.O. Box 22127
Tampa 33622

Miami-Dade Junior College
11380 N.W. 27th Avenue
Miami 33167

Palm Beach Junior College
4200 Congress Street
Lake Worth 33460

St. Petersburg Junior College
St. Petersburg 33710

Valencia Junior College
P.O. Box 3082
Orlando 32809

Georgia

Morris Brown College
643 Hunter Street N.W.
Atlanta 30314

Hawaii

Kapiolani Com. College
620 Pensacola Street
Honolulu 96814

Univ. of Hawaii at Manoa
School of Travel Industry
  Management
1300 Lower Campus Road
Honolulu 96822

Illinois

William Rainey Harper College
510 W. Elk Grove Blvd.
Elk Grove Village 60007

Indiana

Indiana Northern Univ.
Box 1000
University Park
Gas City 46933

Purdue University
Lafayette 47907

Univ. of Notre Dame
Hayes-Healy Travel Manage-
  ment Program
College of Business Admin.
Notre Dame 46556

Iowa

Iowa State Univ.
Ames 50010

Maine

Southern Maine Vocational-
  Technical Institute
Fort Road
South Portland 04106

Washington County Vocational-
  Technical Institute
River Road
Calais 04619

Maryland

Com. College of Baltimore
2901 Liberty Heights Avenue
Baltimore 21215

Hagerstown Jr. College
751 Robinwood Drive
Hagerstown 21740

Montgomery College
51 Mannakee
Rockville 20805

Univ. of Maryland
Dept. of Food, Nutrition,
  and Institutional Admin.
College Park   20742

Massachusetts
Univ. of Massachusetts
Amherst   01002

Michigan
Educational Institute of the
  American Hotel & Motel
  Association (home study and
  group study)
Michigan State Univ.
East Lansing   48823

Ferris State College
Big Rapids   49307

Genesee Com. College
1401 East Court Street
Flint   48503

Michigan State Univ.
School of Hotel, Restaurant, and
  Institutional Management
Eppley Center
East Lansing   48824

Northwood Institute
Box 1526
Midland   48640

Oakland Com. College
27055 Orchard Lake Road
Farmington   48024

Schoolcraft College
18600 Haggerty Road
Livonia   48151
Washtenaw Com. College
P.O. Box 345
Ann Arbor   48107

Minnesota
Southwest Minnesota State
  College

Marshall   56258
Univ. of Minnesota Technical
  College
Crookstone   56716

Missouri
Crowder College
Neosho   64850

Forest Park Com. College
5600 Oakland
St. Louis   63110

Penn Valley Com. College
560 Westport Road
Kansas City   64111

Univ. of Missouri
Columbia   65201

Nebraska
Central Nebraska Vocational-
  Technical School
Box 1024
Hastings   68901

Nevada
Univ. of Nevada
College of Hotel Admin.
Las Vegas   89154

New Hampshire
Thompson School of Applied
  Science
Durham   03824
Univ. of New Hampshire
Durham   03820

New Jersey
Middlesex County College
Edison   08817

New York
Cornell University
School of Hotel Admin.
Statler Hall
Ithaca   14853

Culinary Institute of
America, Inc.
North Road
Hyde Park 12601

Erie Com. College
Main & Youngs Road
Buffalo 14221

Monroe Com. College
410 Alexander Street
Rochester 14607

New York City Com. College
300 Jay Street
Brooklyn 11201

Paul Smith's College
Paul Smiths 12970

Pratt Institute
215 Ryerson Street
Brooklyn 11205

Rochester Institute of
Technology
1 Lomb Memorial Drive
Rochester 14623

Schenectady Com. College
Washington Avenue
Schenectady 12019

State Univ. Agricultural and
Technical College
Cobleskill 12034

State Univ. Agricultural and
Technical College
Delhi 13753

State Univ. Agricultural and
Technical College
Morrisville 13408

State Univ. Agricultural and
Technical College
Wellsville 14895

Sullivan County Com. College
South Fallsburg 12779

North Carolina
Applachian State Univ.
Box 200
Boone 28607

Wilkes Com. College
Drawer 120
Wilkesboro 28697

Ohio
Cuyahoga Com. College
2214 E. 14th Street
Cleveland 44115

Ohio State Univ.
1787 Neil Avenue
Columbus 43210

Oklahoma
Oklahoma State Univ.
School of Hotel and
Restaurant Admin.
Stillwater 74074

Oregon
Portland Com. College
12000 S.W. 49th Avenue
Portland 97219

Pennsylvania
Bucks County Com. College
Swamp Road
Newton 18940

Com. College of Philadelphia
23 S. 11th Street
Philadelphia 19107

Drexel Institute of Tech.
Philadelphia 19104

Lehigh County Com. College
Schnecksville 18104

Luzerne County Com. College
Wilkes Barre 18702

Pennsylvania State Univ.
University Park 16802

Williamsport Area Com. College
1005 W. Third Street
Williamsport 17701

Rhode Island
Bryant College
154 Hope Street
Providence 02906

South Carolina
Univ. of South Carolina
Columbia 29208

South Dakota
South Dakota State Univ.
College of Home Economics
Brookings 57006

Texas
Amarillo College
P.O. Box 447
Amarillo 79105

Del Mar College
101 Baldwin Street
Corpus Christi 78404

El Centro College
Main & Lamar Streets
Dallas 75202

Univ. of Houston
Hilton School of Hotel and
 Restaurant Management
925 Caroline
Houston 77004

Utah
Utah Technical College
Provo 84601

Virgin Islands
College of the Virgin
 Islands
P.O. Box 1826
Charlotte Amalie
St. Thomas 00801

Washington
Seattle Com. College
1625 Broadway
Seattle 98122

Washington State Univ.
Pullman 99163

Wisconsin
District 1—Technical Institute
620 Clairemont Avenue
Eau Claire 54701

Madison Area Tech. College
211 N. Carroll Street
Madison 53703

Milwaukee Technical College
1015 N. 6th Street
Milwaukee 53203

University of Wisconsin—
 Stout
Hotel and Restaurant
 Management Dept.
Menomonie 54751

TOURISM AND TRAVEL MANAGEMENT

California
Los Angeles Trade-Technical
 College
Los Angeles 90015

Mount San Antonio College
Walnut 91789

Colorado
Mesa College
Grand Junction 81501

Univ. of Denver
2030 East Evans Street
Denver 80210

Connecticut
Univ. of New Haven
300 Orange Avenue
West Haven 06516

Florida
Florida International Univ.
School of Hotel, Food, and
  Travel Services
Tamiami Trail
Miami 33144

Florida State Univ.
Hotel and Restaurant Admin.
College of Business
Tallahassee 32306

Hawaii
Univ. of Hawaii at Manoa
School of Travel Industry
  Management
Honolulu 96822

Chaminade College of
  Honolulu
Honolulu 96816

Illinois
Parks College of St. Louis Univ.
Institute of Transportation,
  Travel & Tourism
Cahokia 62206

Indiana
Univ. of Notre Dame
Hayes-Healy Travel Manage-
  ment Program
College of Business Admin.
Notre Dame 46556

Michigan
Educational Institute of the
American Hotel & Motel
Association (for individual
and group study)
Michigan State Univ.
East Lansing 48823

Michigan State Univ.
School of Hotel, Restaurant,
and Institutional Manage-
ment
East Lansing 48824

Nevada
Univ. of Nevada
College of Hotel Admin.
Las Vegas 89154

New York
Adelphi University
Transportation, Travel, and
  Tourism Program
School of Business Admin.
Garden City 11530

Genesee Com. College
Batavia 14020

Herkimer County Com. College
Herkimer 13357

Niagara University
Institute of Transportation,
  Travel, and Tourism
Niagara University 14109

Paul Smith's College
Hotel and Resort Manage-
  ment Dept.
Paul Smiths 12970

Rhode Island
Johnson & Wales College
Providence 02903

TRANSPORTATION

Alabama
  Auburn University
  Auburn 36830
  Univ. of Alabama
  University 35486

Arizona
  Univ. of Arizona
  Tucson 85721

California
  Canada College
  Redwood City 94061

  College of San Mateo
  San Mateo 94402

  De Anza College
  Cupertino 95014

  Foothill College
  Los Altos Hills 94022

  Fresno City College
  Fresno 93704

  Golden Gate College
  San Francisco 94105

  Los Angeles City College
  Los Angeles 90029

  Los Angeles Trade-Technical
   College
  Los Angeles 90015

  Merritt College
  Oakland 94609

  Mira Costa College
  Oceanside 92054

  San Bernardino Valley College
  San Bernardino 92403

San Diego Evening College
San Diego 92101

San Francisco State College
San Francisco 94132

San Jose City College
San Jose 95114

Connecticut
  Yale University
  New Haven 06520

District of Columbia
  American University
  Washington DC 20016

  Georgetown University
  Washington DC 20007

Hawaii
  Univ. of Hawaii at Manoa
  Honolulu 96822

Illinois
  City College of Chicago—
   Kennedy-King College
  Chicago 06021

  City Colleges of Chicago—
   Southwest College
  Chicago 06052

  Lewis & Clark Com. College
  Godfrey 62035

  Moraine Valley Com. College
  Palos Hills 60482

  Parks College of St. Louis
   Univ.
  Cahokia 62206

  Prairie State College
  Chicago Heights 60411

Waubonsee Com. College
Sugar Grove 60554

Indiana
Tristate College
Angola 46703

Univ. of Notre Dame
Notre Dame 46556

Kentucky
Univ. of Louisville
Louisville 40208

Louisiana
Louisiana State Univ.
Baton Rouge 70803

Maryland
Essex Com. College
Baltimore County 21237

Univ. of Baltimore
Baltimore 21201

Michigan
Davenport College of Business
Grand Rapids 49502

Michigan State Univ.
East Lansing 48824

Minnesota
Austin State Junior College
Austin 55912

Mississippi
Mississippi State Univ.
State College 39762

Missouri
Univ. of Missouri
Kansas City 64110

New York
Adelphi Univ.
Garden City 11530

City Univ. of New York—
Queensborough Com. College
Bayside 11364

Columbia University
New York 10027

Niagara University
Niagara University 14109

Polytechnic Institute of
New York
Brooklyn 11201

State Univ. of New York—
Agricultural & Technical
College at Alfred Univ.
Alfred 14802

State Univ. of New York—
Hudson Valley Com. College
Troy 12180

Syracuse University
Syracuse 13210

North Carolina
Univ. of North Carolina
Wilmington 28401

Ohio
Univ. of Akron
Akron 44304

Cuyahoga Com. College
Cleveland 44115

Kent State Univ.
Kent 44242

Ohio State Univ.
Columbus 43210

Oregon
Univ. of Oregon
Eugene 97403

Pennsylvania
Robert Morris College
Pittsburgh 15219

Univ. of Pennsylvania
Philadelphia 19104

Tennessee
East Tennessee State Univ.
Johnson City 37602

Univ. of Tennessee
Knoxville 37916

Virginia
Univ. of Richmond
Richmond 23173

Washington
Green River Com. College
Auburn 98002

Highline Com. College
Midway 98031

Univ. of Washington
Seattle 98105

INDEX